INDIA
A Colourful Kaleidoscope

Julie

So that you always
remember me, and our
hectic weeks in the east
Remember me forever

Loads of Love
Andrew

Copyright © BRIJBASI PRINTERS PVT. LTD.

Published by Brijbasi Printers Pvt. Ltd.
E-46/11, Okhla Industrial Area, Phase II,
New Delhi-110 020.

Published 1992

Editor : MONISHA MUKUNDAN

Designed by : GOPI GAJWANI

Coordinator : R. S. PRAGALBH

Phototypeset by : Alphabets, New Delhi

Printed and bound in Singapore

ISBN 81-7107-030-2

INDIA
A Colourful Kaleidoscope

CONTENTS

Introduction

MONISHA MUKUNDAN

Left: Women in rural Rajasthan wear heavy silver jewellery. Above: A folk painting of Lord Krishna.

Women dressed in vivid-hued skirts, their scarlet and yellow veils billowing around them as they ride to a local fair on a tractor; a satellite being taken to its launching pad on a bullock-cart; women doctors, lawyers and engineers who carry their professional achievements as gracefully as their saris and continue to nurture traditions they value; churches and temples, mosques and Buddhist monasteries, concrete highrises and exquisitely fashioned mud huts . . . the images evoked by India follow one another in rapid succession; contradictory, varied, encompassing several centuries all at once.

Which brings us to the great danger that lies in writing about or photographing India. For every truth, there is an opposite and equally valid truth and the resilience of India's people stems perhaps from their ability to accept and function within the patterns of such contradictions. Rejecting absolutes both in philosophy and in daily life, most Indians understand the ephemeral, constantly changing nature of all that seems immutable. Such an attitude of acceptance, often decried in the West as a sense of fatalism and inertia, gives them the inner strength to deal with an existence that spans many centuries, that supports lives lived at several levels and on seemingly conflicting planes.

An ambitious, highly qualified computer professional may function at a technological level of competence that matches the best in his or her field anywhere in the world. And yet, when it comes to shifting into a new house, that same professional will defer to a parental wish to choose an astrologically auspicious day and time, without any sense of dissonance. Does this create inner conflicts? Perhaps it does. Or possibly, conflicts only arise in minds which perceive everything in absolute terms.

Not so long ago, at a hotel in the fortified desert city of Jaisalmer, a group of Indian visitors began to chat with a young Swiss couple at the next table. The young couple were on a ten-day tour of India and seemed glad of an opportunity to talk to local people, other than guides and hotel staff. Soon an atmosphere of friendly companionship had been established. "Tell us," said the young woman hesitantly, "If you do not mind, please tell us how it is that young Indians still accept marriages arranged by their parents?" She paused and added shyly, "Please, were your marriages arranged?"

"We had a love-marriage, just as you probably did," one Indian couple answered. "Ours was an arranged marriage," another young man volunteered, looking amused.

"Yes?"

"Well, let me put it this way. You had your courtship before you were married.

We had ours after our wedding. And because our parents had chosen carefully, keeping in mind our backgrounds and suitability to each other, our courtship ended in an enduring marriage which may have a more durable base than many Western marriages," he said.

It no longer seemed such an outlandish concept. The European couple nodded, perhaps beginning to gain an insight into the possibility of there being many paths to the same goal, a concept that is familiar in India because of the philosophical base of Hinduism, with its infinite tolerance towards all forms of beliefs and religious practice. In philosophy as in life there is seldom much that is black or white.

And, in more literal terms, there is seldom much that is black or white in an Indian setting either. If it is possible to make any generalisation at all about India, it may be true to say that almost every Indian loves colour and uses it with a felicity that fills the varied Indian landscapes with vivid rainbow hues. But, this being India, there are exceptions even to such a generalisation. In the southern state of Kerala, where Nature has filled the undulating terrain with foliage in every shade of green, where flowers bloom in unbridled intensities of colour and the earth itself is a deep shade or red; the people wear white. In that setting of opulent tropical splendour, even women wear white, a colour shunned in other parts of the country because of its association with widowhood.

Across the border, in the state of Tamil Nadu, colours come into their own once again and find expression not only in clothes but in larger-than-life film hoardings that dominate the streets of Madras, the state capital, and one of India's major metropolises. Madras is also the city in which the British first established their base in India, and remnants of the past remain, in architecture, in commercial organisations, educational institutions, and in a host of other ways.

Kerala, Tamil Nadu, Karnataka, Andhra Pradesh and Maharashtra make up the southern peninsula of the Indian sub-continent. On the west coast, the Arabian Sea has served as a link to the rest of the world for centuries. There was a brisk trade with ancient Rome in the early years of the Christian era. In fact, it is believed that Jesus Christ's disciple, Thomas Didymus, (Doubting Thomas) came to India after Christ's death to preach His gospel. Kerala's Syrian Christians trace the history of their church back to St. Thomas and, in Madras, St. Thomas Mount commemorates the hilltop on which he is said to have been martyred.

Traders from Arabia, China and Persia sailed regularly to India and the ways in which they influenced the people of this region may still be seen in a myriad ways. Chinese-style fishing nets in Cochin in Kerala, the universally used kadai, a vessel which closely resembles the Chinese wok, architecture and innumerable linguistic connections remain to remind us of times past.

In the north, despite the protective barrier of the Himalayas, the highest mountains in the world, wave after wave of invaders crossed high mountain passes and poured down the prosperous and fertile Gangetic Valley. The Aryans came this way about five thousand years ago. Later, the Greeks came, under Alexander the Great, and so did the Turks, the Mongols, the Huns and the Afghans. Closer to our time, European seafaring powers; the Portuguese and the Dutch, the French and the British used the oceans as their passage to India. Each group left something of their culture behind and each took something of India back with them. The exchange enriched both parties and present-day India is a rich and varied tapestry of all the strands which have been woven together to create the fabric of its being.

While the twentieth century explosion of technology has transformed the entire world and far-reaching developments have changed the face of India, life in scattered villages and remote tribal settlements has escaped the overwhelming standardisation of the international consumer culture. Despite the invasion of the electronic media, despite ambitious and enterprising advertising campaigns that reach far-flung habitations, the rooted rhythms of rural life tend to go on as they have always done.

To students of the past as much as to those who seek to understand the present, India offers a fascinating wealth of material and experiences. People of virtually every race and religion call India home. They speak fifteen major languages and hundreds of dialects. They live in landscapes that vary from cold, high altitude deserts to tropical coastal regions, and from riverine valleys to verdant mountains. Each community has its own individuality, for India has always taken pride in the concept of 'unity in diversity' rather than that of a 'melting pot' sameness.

Almost every social and economic system and every ecological environment is in the process of rapid change, with unforseeable results. Even the patterns of the past are undergoing re-assessment as recent archaeological excavations bring startling new evidence to light. And yet, the vitality of India's people finds expression in their ability to transcend their circumstances, and to draw upon a shared pool of creativity and identity. In impoverished villages on the edge of the desert, women still find the time to decorate their mud walls with paintings of amazing beauty and freshness. Their more affluent counterparts in the city also decorate their homes in traditional ways for special festivals and it is not unusual to find auspicious mango leaves strung across the doorway of a city home or a rice-flour decoration traced across a threshold. In the most humble home, the tradition of hospitality will prompt a householder to share a simple meal with a visitor. Life is hard and filled with unimaginable drudgery, but there is still time to sing and to celebrate.

At the other end of the scale are those whose wealth and concerns would be familiar to their counterparts in the West, whose lives revolve around corporate strategy and the compulsions of business, and whose homes and families would blend easily into any affluent neighbourhood in the world. Their's is a life of high fashion and glitter, of discotheques, designer clothes and jet setting holidays, where an individual may spend in an hour what an entire family of construction workers earn in several months.

And, within the parameters of these extremes are a staggering range of other individuals; teachers and scientists, social workers and artists, business executives and classical dancers and musicians who devote themselves to an ancient art that is still vibrantly alive. Each of them has a reality of their own and the visitor to India may choose to enter a plane that differs from that of every other visitor to this land.

Any writing on India and any book on this sub-continent can, at the very best, only offer the reader a fragment of the reality of India. And it is this that makes India so endlessly fascinating, both to those who see it from afar and those who live within its boundaries. For the magic of India lies in its constantly evolving, constantly changing kaleidoscope of simultaneous realities.

The Himalayas
Abode of the Gods
SERBJEET SINGH

Left: Neelkantha Peak, named after Lord Shiva, is part of the high Himalayas. These snow-bound ranges are the highest mountains in the world. Above: Ladakhi women treasure their traditional turquoise-studded head-dresses.

Many years ago, during a trek in the Chamba Lahoul valley of Himachal Pradesh, we were camping below a rocky ledge and all of us in the group were busy preparing our meal for the day. All of a sudden, as if out of nowhere, a sadhu, a religious mendicant, appeared. He was scantily dressed and carried a staff shaped like a trident. He readily accepted our invitation to partake of our meal and, planting his trident in the ground, he started eating. He did not utter a word. Having finished his meal, he got up, took up his trident, looked in the direction of the upper valley ahead as if computing the distance on an imaginary compass and then, shouting "Alakh Niranjan, Jai Shivaji ki" he started off. I got up and asked him where he had come from. Prompt came the reply, "Does any of us know where we come from?" I ventured to enquire where he was going. "Do any of us know where we are going ?" said the holy man and then he marched rapidly away.

This sadhu was one of the thousands who traverse the far-off valleys and passes of the great Himalaya year after year, staying on the outskirts of villages or even in the open, in conditions of incredible hardship. Most of them are followers of various cults that centre around Shiva, the god of the Himalayas.

After this chance meeting with the holy man, we broke camp and started to climb towards the pass ahead. All of a sudden, around a bend, I came face to face, for the first time in my life, with the Great Himalaya . . . ten thousand feet of rock suspended in the sky, with ice and snow clinging to impossible slopes and higher up, a crown of glistening ice piercing the blue skies. It was the west face of Baihali, a 6000-metre summit in the Chamba Lahoul valley. There are, in the twenty-five hundred kilometres of the Great Himalaya Range, about two thousand peaks of over 6000 metres, about a hundred that rise to 7000 metres and then the kings, members of the 7000-8800 metre club.

The Great Himalaya Range skirts north India and its crescent-shaped thrust towards the west, north-west, is the main body of the greatest mountain chain on earth. Celebrated in mythology and religion, the Great Himalaya is said to be the abode of the gods, a veritable pantheon of the Hindu "devas". Unlike places in other climes where mythological nomenclature is a thing of the past, the Himalayas have hundreds of living, functioning shrines and pilgrim destinations that have been so for the last three thousand years. The *Skandha Purana*, Hindu scriptures that date back twenty-five centuries, says:

> As the dew is dried up by the rays of the morning sun,
> So do all sins vanish by the sight of the Himalaya.

In the east is the geographical starting point of this great range. Namche Barwa, a solitary pyramid of rock and ice stands 7756 metres high and around it the Tsangpo river of Tibet tumbles down into Assam where it is known as the mighty Brahmaputra. Further west, along the Great Himalaya Range, are the mighty peaks of Arunachal Pradesh that crown the watershed between Tibet and India. On the slopes of this range is the maze of valleys of Arunachal Pradesh, mainly the basins of the Subansiri and Kameng rivers. These valleys, inhabited by tribal peoples, contain fauna and flora ranging from the tropical to the alpine. The wild fern of the steaming tropical jungles gives way to oak, fir and pine and then the treeline ends at 3000 metres, leading to vast grassy slopes, and then a terrain of rock and snow, ice and glacier. The Dafla and Miri tribes inhabit these valleys of Arunachal Pradesh which are only now being gradually opened to tourists. Along and Passighat on the Brahmaputra river are pilgrim centres and the site of annual fairs. Tucked away in a side valley in the far eastern corner of the Brahmaputra basin is another pilgrim centre for Hindus, Parasuram Kund. Further west, in Arunachal Pradesh, as the Great Himalaya reaches Bhutan, is Buddhist country and the first of the great Buddhist monasteries of the Himalaya is located here at Towang. Then you emerge into the Kingdom of Bhutan and the majestic mountains of Kula Kangri and Chomo Lhari which guard the main valleys of Bhutan. All these valleys are parallel and open up towards the south. Bhutan is dotted with dzongs or fortresses and monasteries. The towns of Thimpu, Punakha and Paro are nestled amidst these steep valleys, hidden in the labyrinth of the Bhutan Himalaya. Bhutan is separated from Sikkim by the Chumbi valley, once the main trading route between India and Tibet.

The basin of the Tista river lies in Sikkim and its northern reaches are dominated by Kanchenjunga, the world's third highest mountain. Fed by glaciers, the many streams of the Tista river tumble through deep gorges, grassy alps and fir forests. Past Gangtok, the main town of Sikkim and the smaller town of Kalimpong, the Tista rushes south into the Indian plains. The famous Buddhist monasteries and pilgrim centres of Sikkim are Rumtek, Yuksom, Tashiding and Pemayangtse.

Further west, in the Nepal Himalaya, is a galaxy of the world's highest mountains, Everest, Makalu, Gauri Shankar, Ganesh Himal, Manasalu, Annapurana, Dhaulagiri. The weird formation of the three Annapurana, summits (all 8000 metres) looks like a huge marble platform, fifteen kilometres across. Beyond Annapurana the Great Himalaya dips down to the Gandak river gorge, making it one of the most fearsome sights in the world, with the range rising on the other side of the gorge to Dhaulagiri. Beyond Dhaulagiri is the maze of mountain systems of Kanjiroba Himal and Api, until you come to the Garhwal Himalaya.

It is in the Garhwal Himalaya that the real "Zeitgeist" of the Hindus is manifest. Garhwal Himalaya, being the source basin of the Ganga, holiest of rivers, has a special place in the folklore and legends of India. It is "Devanbhoomi", the abode of the gods. If you were to start your journey into the Garhwal Himalayas from Rishikesh, where the holy river Ganga emerges from the Himalayas into the plains of India, going upstream along the blue-green waters of the Ganga, you would come upon the pilgrim town of Devaprayag. It is a tiny hamlet clinging to a steep cliff with temples and shelters all over the mountainside. Here the Alaknanda river, coming from the east Garhwal Himalaya joins the Bhagirathi, coming from the west Garhwal Himalaya to form the mighty Ganga.

It is early morning at Devaprayag and on a stone platform above the thundering river stands a pilgrim. He takes hold of a fixed iron chain and then takes a dip in the raging waters uttering "Har Har Mahadev Shambho . . . Kashi Viswanath Ganga". This is a supreme moment for the pilgrim, who, like nearly two million others, makes the journey to Badrinath, Kedarnath and Gangotri at the headwaters of the Ganga. Here, along the pilgrim route, the blue-green waters of the Mandakini river pour into the Alaknanda. Now the pilgrim route to Badrinath starts the ascent to higher altitudes. Through side valleys you get an occasional glimpse of the great spurs with snowbeds visible from behind dizzying rock faces. You get a feeling of being in the proximity of the Great Himalaya itself. Beyond Joshimath, a pilgrim destination, the ascent to Badrinath starts in a canyon. There is roaring water everywhere: streams big and small pouring their blue waters into the Alaknanda. The treeline is now left behind and at Hanuman Chatti (where the legendary monkey god, Hanuman is said to have humbled a warrior of yore) the final ascent begins. Suddenly you emerge on to a vast open valley surrounded by gigantic mountain peaks. A signboard reads "Devabhoomi Badrinath" (Abode of the God, Badrinath). The little township of Badrinath stands on a rock escarpment overlooking the Alaknanda. The saffron coloured standard of the gods flutters from the dome of the shrine at Badrinath. All round this spot, mountains are visible close at hand, their summits rising above the lesser ridges, Kamet . . . Badrinath . . . Neelkantha. Tens of thousands of pilgrims come to Badrinath every summer from all corners of India. Badrinath, one of the holiest shrines for all Hindus, was founded by the seventh century sage from South India, Adi Shankara, who expounded the Advaita (Monism) school of Hindu thought, popularly known as Vedanta. Legend has it that Lord Vishnu, the Preserver, was seen by the god Shiva enjoying the salubrious climes of these regions in the company of his consort Lakshmi. Whereupon Shiva taunted Vishnu for being given to luxury in a place meant for meditation. It is said that thereafter Vishnu went into meditation at this spot for one million years, eating only alpine grass that grows at these altitudes (Badri grass). Hence the name Badrinath. Behind the temple town of Badrinath is the famed summit of Neelkantha, seemingly so close at hand that you feel as if its hanging glaciers are about to tumble over into the valley below. The mountains of the east Garhwal Himalaya are the testing ground for many an intrepid mountaineer. Kamet has been climbed many times. Nanda Devi, further east, towers above a fantastic landscape – a basin enclosed on three sides. The Nanda Devi basin has been closed in recent years for mountaineers and declared a sanctuary. The summit of Nanda Devi is visible from hundreds of kilometres all around.

If you were to come back into the main Ganga valley at Devaprayag, on the western side of the Garhwal Himalaya, you could go upstream on another famous pilgrim trail towards Gaumukh, past Uttarkashi and on to Tapovan. This is literally a glen for meditation as the Sanskrit name suggests. Many holy men and pilgrims from all parts of India meditate here amidst glistening rocks that hem the sacred Ganga from all sides. Beyond, the pilgrim trail leads to Gangotri, a famous temple site. Then you ascend further, higher and higher until you come upon a remarkable scene. At 4500 metres you are face to face with Gaumukh (literally, cow's mouth) the actual source of the Ganga at the tip of the Gangotri glacier. Water rushes forth from the mouth of the glacier and pilgrims are seen everywhere. Water from here is carried by pilgrims to their homes in all corners of India. "Ganga Jal" (Ganga water) is said to be the ultimate purifier. It is given to new born babies. It is put in the mouths of dying Hindus.

The Gangotri glacier is a sea of ice almost thirty kilometres long. All around is a vast concourse of moraine, icefalls and smaller glaciers issuing forth from the legendary mountains that form a circle around Gangotri. Shivling, the three peaks of Bhagirathi I, Bhagirathi II and Bhagirathi III. Truly, this seems the place where the Ganga issued from the locks of Shiva's hair. Between the valleys of Badrinath and Gangotri, lies the high valley of the Mandakini river. At the headwaters of this river stands the temple of Kedarnath, a thousand-year-old stone structure in the "chhatri" style of the Himalayas. Kedarnath is one of the holiest of pilgrim destinations. It is said that when Shiva cursed the Mahabharata heroes for having slaughtered their kin, the Pandavas sought his pardon but Shiva disappeared from Varanasi and went to Kedarnath and hid himself there. The Pandavas, however, followed him thither and they were granted pardon. Thereafter, the Pandavas are said to have ascended to heaven from a rock cliff outside Kedarnath known as Mahapanth. Till the nineteenth century this rock was the scene of suicides by many old people who sought salvation.

Beyond Garhwal, the Great Himalaya leaps northwest, breaking into many ranges and high valleys, until it is cut by the deep defile of the Satluj river, that comes from Tibet and enters India at Shipki La. Further north, the great Himalaya towers over Spiti, a district of Himachal Pradesh. This is Buddhist country and Kye is the first lamasery in these parts. The people of Spiti are a mixture of Ladakhi and Pahari stock and are traders and small farmers. At Kunzum La you enter the land of Lahoul. In the triangle formed between the two streams of the Chandra and the Bhaga, later to become Chandrabhaga downstream, there is a fantastic outcrop of over fifty snow peaks, the famous CB group of peaks in geographer's parlance. This group of Lahoul peaks is a mountaineers' paradise. Lahoul is Buddhist country and a few small lamaseries dot the valley. Beyond the confluence of the Chandra and the Bhaga near the town of Keylong, the Chandrabhaga as one stream rushes through a gorge, and then through wild scenery for about two hundred and fifty kilometres, until it emerges in Kishtwar as the mighty Chenab river.

Meanwhile, the march of the great Himalaya continues and its western bastion, south of Lahoul, contains the Shigri glacier with its ice walls rising to 6000 metres. Below, to the west, lies the Kulu Valley known as the "valley of the gods". Legend has it that once upon a golden afternoon in the heyday of mythological aeons, Shiva the god of the Himalayas was crossing the Hampta pass from Shigri glacier to the Kulu valley. Shiva was accompanied by his consort, the goddess Parvati, who was carrying in a basket three hundred and sixty-five lesser deities. A chance blizzard at the pass caused the basket to fall and the lid to open. Out flew the three hundred odd "deotas", and these gods settled in the three hundred and sixty-five villages of Kulu. Ever since that day, the people of these villages take their gods in procession and proceed to the grand concourse of the gods at Kulu during the Dussehra festival in autumn. On the last day of the festival all the gods are led in a procession by the chief "deota", Raghunath Ji. In the days preceding this festival, the surrounding forests resound to the sound of processions coming in from the villages, with the gods carried in palanquins by villagers. Kettle drums and horns herald the advent of the gods into Kulu, accompanied by their devotees.

North-west and west of Kulu, a mountain range known as Dhaula Dhaar (the white haired range) bifurcates from the main Himalaya and turns south and then sharply north-west. The Dhaula Dhaar range divides the famed Kangra valley to the south and Chamba to the north. The granite summits of Dhaula Dhaar emerge abruptly from the Kangra Valley floor. On its southern slopes is the town of Dharmsala, the abode of the fourteenth Dalai Lama of Tibet. Dharmsala has become a destination for Buddhist pilgrims from all over the world. In the lamasery at Dharmsala, there exists the world's only school of Buddhist Dialectics, Theckchen Choeling, where lama students can be seen debating in the open garden every afternoon. When the morning prayer starts in the Dalai Lama's main chapel, a hundred sonorous voices of the Buddhist Choir create a strange atmosphere and from the windows, the mighty Dhaula Dhaar with its snowfields and rock pinnacles seems close at hand.

Below Dharmsala, the Kangra Valley stretches for a hundred kilometres. Kangra is celebrated in Indian legend and folklore. It is the home of the world-famous "Pahari" school of miniature painting. Many festivals and fairs are held all over the Kangra valley specially at Jwalamukhi, where a flame rises from subterranean rock. Many forts of the Rajput rulers of the past can be seen all over Kangra Valley, built atop rock eminences or by the side of the Beas river.

In the north, across the Dhaula Dhaar range is Chamba, one of the oldest Hindu kingdoms from the seventh century. The town of Chamba stands on a plateau overlooking the Ravi and has almost five hundred temples, big and small. Every year this quaint town, overshadowed by the Raja's palace, is the scene of a seven-day festival, the Minjar festival, when there is much dancing and merrymaking and drinking, with plenty of local brew on hand. About seventy kilometres upstream from Chamba is the ancient town of Brahmaur, the homeland of the Gaddis, the shepherds of the high hills. At Brahmaur is the Chaurassi, a complex of eighty-four temples. Brahmaur is the starting point of an annual pilgrimage in autumn, when thousands make the steep ascent to a small lake below Mount Manimahesh, the golden throne of Shiva. North of Chamba, the great Himalaya continues north-westwards with incredibly high mountain passes allowing the only passage across it to Zanskar in Ladakh. Beyond the Great Himalaya is the northern shield of the valley of Kashmir. The crowning peaks of the Himalaya here are the twin summits of Nun (7135 metres) and Kun (7077 metres).

South of this and contained in the crescent-like sweep of the Pir Panjaal range is the vale of Kashmir, with its lakes, placid river, vistas of trees, forested ranges and snow peaks – a veritable paradise on earth. The handsome Kashmiri people with their amazing craft skills, have passed the craft from one generation to the other by the "Taalim" process. "Taalim" literally means education but it is used to define carpet designs, traditional motifs and weaving processes. In the side valley of Pahlgam is the route to the famous Amarnath cave where an ice "lingam" or phallic symbol of Lord Shiva is formed every year in a cave where thousands congregate. On the other side of the Pahlgam valley is the Sind valley closed in by the Zoji La, lowest of the great Himalaya passes. Across the Zoji La you experience, within a few kilometres, the golden haze and bleak landscape of high Asia. You enter Ladakh and the fabled monasteries of Mulbekh, Lamayuru, Alchi, Shey, Tiksey and Hemis, which stand on mountain tops with prayer flags fluttering on the topmost storeys. This is trans Himalaya or Little Tibet. Ladakh is utterly different from anything else in the Himalayas. North of Ladakh is the mighty Karakoram Range with the world's largest glaciers, most fearsome rock faces and 7500 to 8800 metre mountains like Saser Kangri and K.2.

Meanwhile, the Great Himalaya range that we left at Zoji La, lurches towards the north-west in a climactic rock and ice formation, terminating in the mighty Nanga Parbat. Nanga Parbat stands alone amongst lesser mountain ranges, a king amongst the barons. As the sun sets on Nanga Parbat, its dazzling icefields, hanging glaciers and sharp summits make a befitting finale to the Great Himalaya Range that started two thousand, five hundred kilometres away with Namche Barwa in the east.

The Garhwal Himalayas in the state of Uttar Pradesh, contain innumerable temples and many places of pilgrimage.

Following page: The high Himalayas draw mountaineers from all over the world.

Left: The shikara, a simple boat is characteristic of Kashmir. Above: A master-craftsman at work on a finely painted papier mâché vase. Kashmiri craftspeople are renowned for their skill and artistry.

Herds of sheep are taken to graze in high altitude meadows in the shadow of the eternal snows in Sikkim.

*Left: Ladakhi women,
wearing their traditional
head-dresses studded with
turquoise, carry offerings to
a Buddhist shrine.
Above: Masked lamas or
Buddhist monks perform
ritual dances at an annual
festival at Rumtek in Sikkim.*

Bhimakali monastery in Sarahan, Himachal Pradesh.

Left: Tso Morari, a large, brackish water lake in Ladakh. Above: A Ladakhi Buddhist turns a prayer wheel. Prayers engraved on the drum and inside it, are believed to be broadcast with each turn of the wheel. Following page: The great Himalayas draw mountaineers and pilgrims from all over the world.

The Gangetic Plain
Along the Sacred River
TEESTA VERMA YADAV

Left: Activities on the ghats of Banaras are largely suspended during the monsoon. Boats are carefully moored out of reach of the turbulent currents in the river. Above: An ash-besmeared sadhu, or religious mendicant beside the river Ganga.

Ganga Mata ki Jai! Praise be to Mother Ganga, proclaimed an old sadhu, standing waist deep in icy cold water. He took a dip in the river and rose dripping out of the water, his hands folded in salutation to the river and to the rising sun as it dispersed the early morning mist. The sadhu, a saffron-clad religious mendicant, and his prayers, characterised the attitude that thousands of Indians share towards the Ganga, the most sacred of all India's rivers. In worshipping the river and the rising sun each morning, this sadhu and all those devout individuals who are to be seen each morning beside the river, express a deep respect for all creation which finds fulfillment in a number of rituals which pay obeisance to the creative and nurturing forces of the earth.

At the foot of the mighty Himalayas, where the Ganga emerges from the mountains, the town of Haridwar rises to the chime of temple bells and the blowing of conch shells, as priests, holy men and pilgrims from all over India gather on the stepped bathing ghats beside the river. Haridwar is considered one of the holiest places on the river and is an object of pilgrimage to devotees from distant corners of the country. This is considered the 'gateway to the gods' and is the starting point for many a strenuous pligrimage into the mountains, to the higher reaches of the holy river and to its source at Gaumukh, where a small and icy stream flows from the eternal snows of the high Himalayas.

In mythology, the Ganga is said to have descended from the heavens, as a boon granted to King Bhagiratha after long and severe penance dedicated to Lord Shiva. Roaring and foaming, the river came down from the heavens with such great force that it would have destroyed the earth had not Shiva broken the force of its descent with his thick and tangled locks of hair. He guided the river through his matted hair, until it fell gently upon the earth. From earliest times, the Ganga has shaped the course of India's history, its scriptures, literature and art. It is deeply rooted in the consciousness of almost every Indian and is central to a great deal of Indian thought, belief and religious ritual. In a predominantly agricultural society, the Ganga was an artery carrying life blood to the plains of a fertile land. It is not surprising that the river is regarded as a goddess, an all-powerful, bountiful Mother, to whom devout Hindus offer their salutations each morning.

The Ganga begins its long journey through the plains of India at the tip of the Gangotri glacier, at a height of 4,225 metres in the Garhwal Himalayas. A temple dedicated to the Goddess Ganga marks its source. From Gaumukh, where the river emerges from the Gangotri glacier are a number of centres of pilgrimage and retreats for ascetics who find inspiration and serenity beside the icy waters of the snow-fed stream at this altitude. The river is called the Bhagirathi here, and, as it flows towards Haridwar, it is joined by the Alaknanda at a place called Devprayag. From here, the two streams flow together as the Ganga.

Stretches of the upper Ganga, Bhagirathi and the Alaknanda, right down to Rishikesh have become popular with adventurers seeking the thrills of kayaking and white water river rafting, and trekking through forests of oak and rhododendron, deodar and pine.

Rafting down the Ganga is an exciting experience over roaring rapids and swirling crests. The river quietens down as it spreads out at Rishikesh, a peaceful and tranquil town, surrounded by a dense tangle of vegetation on the surrounding slopes of the Shivaliks which create an image of a sage's matted locks, thereby giving the place its name. The suspension bridge Laxman Jhoola, literally, Laxman's swing spans the Ganga, marking the end of a thrilling rafting run. Rishikesh is known for its religious retreats, its ashrams and Yoga Centres, where solace seekers from all over the world come to spend their time in meditation and repose. The Shivananda Ashram and the Geeta Bhavan are important centres, where discourses are held on Hindu religious texts.

It is at Haridwar that the river finally descends to the plains and begins its journey through the state of Uttar Pradesh, towards the east, through the neighbouring states of Bihar and Bengal to keep its tryst with the Bay of Bengal. Haridwar is amongst the holiest places of pilgrimage in India. Temples, hermitages and dharamsalas line the banks of the Ganga. According to legend, Haridwar is said to have been sanctified by the three deities of the Hindu pantheon – Brahma, Vishnu and Shiva. Har-Ki-Pauri has a footprint on stone, which is said to be that of Lord Vishnu. In the evenings, the aarti or worship with lamps at this ghat is an elevating experience. Lighted earthen lamps are set afloat down the river to the accompaniment of temple bells and religious music.

Every twelve years, Haridwar plays host to thousands of pilgrims from all over the country who come here to participate in the Kumbha Mela. However, the greatest and most important Kumbha Mela is held every sixth and twelfth year at Prayag (Allahabad). The city's supreme sanctity as the confluence of the Ganga, Yamuna and the mythical Saraswati, is accentuated by the story behind the gathering. After wresting the jar (kumbha) of immortal nectar from the demons, a god in the form of a rook flew with it to paradise. Prayag was one of the places he rested. The journey took twelve days. Since each divine day is considered equivalent to twelve earth years, the cycle was established. One "ardh" (half) Kumbha occurs every six years. A large congregation of pilgrims, saints, sages and crowds unparalleled anywhere else in the world gathers to take a dip in the holy Ganga.

Before meeting the Yamuna halfway down the plains, the Ganga passes by the city of Kanpur, the major industrial centre of Uttar Pradesh, known for its manufacture of fine quality leather and textile goods. Cities, towns and villages cover the Gangetic basin, one of the world's largest alluvial tracts and the most densely populated. This is fertile farmland, nurtured by the river.

In addition to the Ganga, the plain is watered by other rivers like the Yamuna, the Ghagra, the Gandak and the Gomti, and their tributaries. The top soil in the river basins is renewed annually with the inundation caused by the monsoons. The Ganga alone is estimated to bring down half a million tonnes of silt and suspended matter daily. Lush green plantations of sugarcane and rice, mustard and wheat flourish in this area. Orchards of mangoes, guavas and other fruit, create islands of dappled shade amidst the fields of this fertile basin.

It is no wonder that the wealth of the fertile Indo-Gangetic plain has determined the course of our history. Since the beginning of Indian civilization there has been tragic repetition of invasions through the north-western Himalayan passes, starting with the arrival of the Aryans over two millenia back.

Kingdoms rose and fell. The Mauryas, the Sungas and the Sakas, the Kushans the Huns and the Guptas. Some looted and left, some stayed on. Thus a fusion of many new and foreign ideas into the existant cultural fabric took place.

The end of the first millenium A.D., saw the advent of Islam in India. After a series of attacks by the Turks and the Arabs, the climax came with the Mughals who left behind indelible marks on Indian life and culture. They were followed by the European powers. The British established their dominion over India in the eighteenth century bringing changes that remain to this day.

The twentieth century brought liberation from foreign domination and the decades since Independence in 1947, have witnessed the transformation of India. A civilization of classical antiquity is in the process of change, into a modern industrial community, demonstrating a remarkable capacity to adapt and develop.

Allahabad, in the present century, is associated with the Nehru family, who have moulded the country's politics for the past forty years. As the sun sets on the past and the western horizon, we take a boat ride to the 'Triveni Sangam' where the river Yamuna and the mythological Saraswati join the Ganga.

About eighty-nine kilometres downstream from Allahabad lies the famous town of Mirzapur, known for its hand-knotted carpets woven by traditional Indian craftsmen. Commanding the highway into Bengal, the historic fort of Chunar stands on the banks of the Ganga. It was here that the Afghan ruler Sher Shah Suri defeated the Mughal Emperor Humayun in the sixteenth century.

Further south is the holiest of all Indian cities, Varanasi, once called Banaras. Early in the morning, long before dawn, temple bells begin to peal across the city. By the ghats on the river Ganga, the waters flow slowly past, carrying garlands of marigold, earthen oil lamps long extinguished by the waves, and religious offerings. As the moments pass, the sky begins to lighten, the chiming of bells rise to a crescendo, and down the narrow lanes of Varanasi come the faithful, those who will bathe here in the holiest of holy rivers and thus purify themselves, those who come to offer prayers, others who wish to renounce the material pleasures of the world, and those who come to perform the last rites of a departed soul.

Faith is the touchstone of Varanasi and religion its temper. The city has attained glory as the centre of Hinduism, the seat of Vedic culture and learning, of commerce and craftsmanship. The Banaras Hindu University and the Kashi University are great seats of learning.

The talents and skills of Varanasi's people are its wealth. Displayed in the tiny shops of its back streets, jostled by crowds of people, sacred cows, bicycles and scooters, are shimmering silks and richly woven brocades, cotton and woollen textiles, brightly coloured bracelets, copperware and jewellery.

The conical gold-spiralled dome of the Kashi Vishwanath along with the Tulsi

Manas and the Bharat Mata Temples dominate the waterfront. The conical shapes penetrate the mist like smoke which rises from the funeral pyres, while birds wheel incessantly above. To a Hindu, death in Varanasi is the most propitious of all, it means the cycle of coming and going has come to an end. The smell of incense wafts from the temples and the boatman sings a haunting lyric as the river laps against the hull of the boat. Amidst the buzz of human voices, temple bells accompanied by the sound of conches strike the ear with a magic melody. As darkness gathers, earthen lamps and marigold flowers are set afloat, as they drift downstream along with the current, a sense of serenity and wonder fills the soul.

Keeping her rendezvous with the Gomti River, the Ganga, wider and muddier than ever, enters the state of Bihar, the cradle of Jainism and Buddhism. Pataliputra or Patna was once the seat of a major Indian dynasty.

Today, Sher Shah's mosque dominates the skyline of the city. Close by stands Harmandir Sahib, a Sikh temple dedicated to their tenth guru, Guru Gobind Singh, who was born in Patna. Alongside is another mosque 'Pathar ki Masjid', next to which is the Hanuman temple and the beehive-like structure of the Golghar built by the British to store grain.

Bihar is the land of the Buddha. Emperor Ashoka of the Mauryan dynasty, who converted to Buddhism and was responsible for the spread of the Buddha's teachings to the Far East, ruled from here. He left an indelible mark on the social, cultural and philosophical history of India.

Nearing journey's end, the Ganga enters Bengal and distributes its waters into two main streams; one of them is the Padma which flows onto Bangladesh and joins the Brahmaputra to form the Gangetic delta. Here the vegetation is lush and the trees of the Sunderbans forests, known for the famous Royal Bengal Tiger, are much taller than those on the Indian side, for the Indian Sunderbans are not fed by a fresh water stream so the mangrove forests growth is rather stunted due to the salt waters coming in from the sea.

The Ganga, which now flows south through West Bengal is known as the Hooghly. Bengal is mentioned in the epic, the Mahabharata and in Ptolemy's geography. It was then a seafaring state, sending traders to Sri Lanka, Sumatra and Java and received visitors from Greece, Persia and China. From the end of the nineteenth century, Bengal was one of the most prosperous territories of the British Empire. A new Bengali culture developed under the Raj. Temples were built, the Bengali language was enriched by poets and writers such as Bankim Chandra Chatterjee and Rabindranath Tagore. Major religious philosophers like Ramakrishna and Vivekananda appeared. Belur Math and the Sri Ramakrishna Temple, headquarters of the Ramakrishna Mission are situated on the Hooghly river.

West Bengal is a living testimony to the milieu of cultures that have crossed the land over the past two hundred years. On the right bank of the Hooghly river, less than sixty kilometres from Calcutta, along the Grand Trunk Road, are sleepy little towns with mansions, palaces, old churches, riverfront promenades, colonial houses and cemeteries – remains of the old Portuguese, Danish, Dutch and French settlements. Serampore, Chandernagore, Chinsura and Bandel along the Hooghly have had their toll of battles, conquests and defeats, for control of the Hooghly once meant control of all the foreign trade that flowed through Bengal. Calcutta is the last major city through which the Ganga flows before submerging her identity with the seas of the Bay of Bengal. Across the Hooghly, is Calcutta, the largest city in the country, with a population of over ten million. Something is always happening here, be it religious celebrations, concerts or political demonstrations, film festivals or soccer matches, horse races or a cricket match, it is a temperamental city with a highly creative people who endow it with its many moods.

The religious fervour during the celebrations of Durga Puja, is unmatched anywhere else in the country. Huge tents are set up with images of the powerful, beautiful and fierce Goddess Durga. Music, poetry and drama are performed before enthralled audiences. The images are carried in triumphant processions to the holy Ganga and are ceremonially immersed on the tenth day of the festival. The river side ghats, like any on the Ganga, are most active at dawn and sunset. During festivals thousands converge on Babu, Outram and Princep Ghats to immerse clay images of Durga, Kali, Laxmi or Saraswati into the river. Other communities hold festivals too. On Chaat, the Sun festival, Biharis dip fruit in the river and Sindhis, on Cheetti Chand, immerse statues of the god Jhulelal. Every morning, the ghats swarm with people taking a holy dip, washing and praying.

In the evenings, lovers stroll on the riverfront promenades or hire a dingy for a ride on the river against the backdrop of Fort William and the gleaming white Victoria Memorial. A visit to Calcutta is not complete without a visit to its many markets. Handloom sarees and Murshidabad silks, gold filigree, conch shell jewellery, jute handicrafts, leather bags, terracotta tiles, the variety is mind boggling. As the Hooghly slowly meanders south, all along the river, ships, trawlers, steamboats and fishing boats pace the waterway in ceaseless activity. Fifty kilometres downstream from Calcutta, the river takes a bend towards the sea, forming a natural harbour. Diamond Harbour was a former stronghold of Portuguese pirates and remains of their fort line the riverfront.

The Ganga finally flows into the Bay of Bengal caressing the island of Sagardwip. The place is so sacred that dying at Sagardwip is believed to be enough to ensure the attainment of nirvana. Every year, in mid-January, a religious festival, Gangasagar Mela, is celebrated here. Over half a million pilgrims gather to take a holy dip and pay homage at the Kapil Muni Temple that washes them clean of their sins.

The orange ball of fire sinks into the sea, all is one, the very essence of all that is India, a process of infinite creation. From the beginning to the end, the journey of the Ganga symbolizes the cycle of life and the spirit and soul of every human being.

*Preceding page: Ghats, or
stepped, paved areas to the
water's edge, line the bank of
the sacred river Ganga at
Banaras.
Left: The temple at Gangotri
in the Garhwal Himalayas,
close to the source of the
sacred river Ganga.
Above: Flowing out of
Gaumukh, the source of the
river, an icy stream of water
cascades over fantastic
formations of rock.*

Above: A sadhu, one of many such holy men who converge on Haridwar for this festival.

Right: Thousands of devotees gather for a dip at Har ki Pauri on the Ganga at Haridwar during the Kumbha Mela, which marks an especially auspicious period once every twelve years.

Heads of religious orders are taken in procession on decorated chariot-cars and sometimes on elephant-back, to participate in the auspicious bath in the river at appointed times during the Kumbha Mela.

Above: Pilgrims seek the help of priests seated under bamboo umbrellas in order to carry out certain religious rituals beside the river at Banaras. Right: A bath in the Ganga is the culmination of many a devout pilgrimage.

Pilgrims dry their saris on the banks of the holy Ganga.

Left: A contemplative moment at dawn beside the Ganga at Banaras. Above: Priests conducting ritual worship in the sanctum of a Shiva temple.

Above: Cow worship in a street in Banaras. In an agricultural country, veneration for cows grew from their importance in the lives of the people. Right: A priest awaits the arrival of pilgrims. In front of him are all the materials he will require to perform religious rituals. Following page: Akash Deep, 'sky lamps' suspended in baskets on long bamboo poles are among the many ritual observances on the banks of the holy Ganga at Banaras. They are believed to light the way across the river of rebirth.

Rajasthan and Gujarat
Royal Palaces and Desert Spaces
KISHORE SINGH

Left: A procession taken out by Muslims during their observance of Moharrum, goes past the Hawa Mahal, 'the palace of the winds' in Jaipur, the capital of Rajasthan. Above: A camel herder.

The desert kings built formidable forts for they were warriors and their kingdoms controlled trade-route revenues. Within the forts, they ordered delicate, fragile palaces. There were temples for their family deities, and beautifully embellished Jain temples, for a vast number of their revenue-collectors and state administrators were of the Jain faith. Their ministers lived in traditional havelis with open courtyards, and separate sections for the zenana where the women gathered and men were not permitted, much as in the palaces. The townspeople, those of humbler origin, used vegetable dyes and skill to adorn their modest homes. Survival was worthy of celebration in the desert, and the architecture of the region personified this attitude.

The origin of desert kingdoms is fairly recent, for the Rajput rulers of the area originally inhabited the fertile plains of India. After losing a number of battles, these proud clans settled in the desert in order to be able to establish their sovereignity once again.

In Rajasthan, they constituted a powerful force, and were close enough to the capital at Delhi (or Agra) to be considered a constant threat to the ruler that controlled the destinies of greater Hindustan. The desert created its own barrier, but the Rajput rulers also used every natural advantage to build their fortified capitals. The first forts came up on the scarps of the Aravallis, that lay like a beam across the desert. Chittaurgarh and Kumbhalgarh were placed on hilltop-plateaux; so was Jodhpur's Mehrangarh as well as the fort at Bundi. From these heights they could control the surrounding plains. Yet Chittaurgarh was sacked a number of times, Kumbhalgarh was lost and Nahargarh too had to succumb.

Other rulers used the hills to establish ramparts that rose upon the contours of the hills and provided natural defenses, as at Amber, the former capital of the Jaipur family; or at Bundi where the ramparts moved in a series of terraces. Still others created their own defences. Bikaner was surrounded by sand, the fort of Junagarh was surrounded by an artificial moat; Jaisalmer used the contours of the golden sand to blend into the ramparts of its golden fort, so the two merged.

Access to these forts was through a series of gateways, so that if one was breached, the next would offer defence against an invader. There were massive gates, made of the sturdiest wood, and driven with pointed nails so elephants could not be used to knock them down. Overlooking the gates and all along the ramparts were vents from where soldiers could pour burning hot oil on those attempting to scale the walls. Entry to the palaces and apartments within the fort were never impressive, but this too served a purpose. Narrow staircases, curving corridors and low doors meant that entry could be regulated, and even one person would be able to hold out against invaders for a sufficiently long time. This enabled members of the royal family to escape into the underground warrens that were so much a part of the fortresses. All forts also featured underground dungeons, and these were used as much for holding political prisoners as for punishing queens who had displeased the maharajas and needed time in isolation to see the error of their ways and seek royal pardon!

Battles and seiges were a winter event; the summer was used for the consolidation of armies, and for building. The Rajputs were also aesthetes, and for them the adornment of their environment was a vital part of their existence. Their palaces often had delicate windows with arches and stone screens to allow in cooling breezes and to offer privacy to the women of the zenana. Coloured glass was used to break the harsh summer light, bathing the rooms in a pleasant, cooling glow. Mirror was used profusely in what came to be referred to as Sheesh Mahal apartments, and almost every royal home had such a Palace of Mirrors, an affectation they acquired from their Mughal neighbours in Delhi and Agra. In fact, formal durbars in opulent surroundings were also a Mughal affectation that the Rajput kings acquired. Like the Mughals, they embellished their own palaces with variations of pietra-dura inlay, often using alabaster and gold paint with such skill, their walls glowed with a life of their own. Artists were offered patronage, and they adorned royal interiors with paintings of the finest quality. These could be portraits of the maharajas, religious paintings – usually of Radha and Krishna, or floral motifs, and they covered entrance archways, walls and ceilings with finely detailed paintings.

Defensive architecture ceased with the first peace treaties with the Mughals, and was almost eliminated under British consolidation. This ended one era of building activities, and generated a second, equally spectacular phase. Gone was the need for fortifications. Palaces stepped out of forts, came into the open, and became architectural entities. It is to this phase that many of Gujarat's palaces belong, with their Renaissance and Italian and even Dutch facades. Those of Rajasthan took more from the soil, and are often more bewitching. The royal family of Udaipur moved away from the fortifications of the City Palace to build a number of palaces on islands in the lake. These were summer pleasure resorts, delicate, fairytale-like, of the purest white marble; the interiors opulently adorned with paintings and lacquerware. There were courtyards with fountains, and boats to ferry the royal family from the City Palace to their summer palaces.

The Kachchawas, the royalty of present-day Jaipur gave up their stronghold of Amber and the rugged fortresses of Jaigarh (with its own gun foundry) and Nahargarh to design themselves a new city. That is how Jaipur came into being three centuries ago. If Amber was tier upon tier of beautiful buildings, Jaipur unfolded according to the tenets of traditional architectural planning as interpreted by the city's chief architect, Vidyadharji. Under the guidance of the astronomer-king, Sawai Jai Singh and with the City Palace complex at the heart of the new capital, Jaipur grew according to a pre-conceived design, with straight roads, a series of markets, observation points for processions and community-held residences. There was ample space for gardens and for ateliers; the familiar Hawa Mahal started off as a temple and was eventually used by the women of the zenana to observe state processions and life in the bazaar below. The city used the pale sandstone of the region for its building, but got its soubriquet of pink city in the tone of an autumnal sunset when it was literally painted pink for the reception of a visiting Prince of Wales. The city integrated Rajput architectural details with Mughal devices in a happy blend that was to be copied later by royal builders all over Rajasthan and much of northern India.

Though the traditional palaces continued to be the residences of most royal families till late in the 19th century, by the turn of this century most families had established more westernized modern residences in the British style. The power of office was no longer in the hands of the princes, and though they attended to the daily administration of their states, there was much more time for leisure. Bikaner established its contemporary Lallgarh Palace in 1901, one of the finest examples of Rajput architecture, using red sandstone and the delicacy of stone-screens very effectively. Yet, the designer of this very Rajput palace was an Englishman, Sir Swinton Jacob, who had done much of his research on Rajput architecture in Jaipur, and refused to blend British design into what he perceived as a very imaginative and purposeful sense of desert architecture.

H.V. Lanchester had no such hesitation when he was commissioned to build the magnificent Umaid Bhawan in Jodhpur. The palace, considered the world's largest private residence, with three hundred and forty seven rooms, has little that is Rajput or even remotely Indian about it. Rajput palaces looked outward and were airy; Lanchester's Umaid Bhawan is inward looking, a building devised not for a warm but a cold climate. It is solid, something it shares with the Mehrangarh Fort; however, it has none of the delicacy of the palaces and apartments within Mehrangarh. It has an imposing majesty, and could well be a government building anywhere in Great Britain. Inside are twin staircases, royal suites, formal apartments, a private auditorium, banquet halls and dining rooms, lounges and collonnaded corridors.

Influences that were strictly localised characterise much of the architecture at Jaisalmer, the 12th century capital of the Bhatti Rajputs. There are Islamic influences, for trade caravans passed through the desert here and gave the state its much-needed revenues. Muslim craftsmen were the major architects and sculptors of the havelis that characterise this city. While the palaces within the fort are dark and brooding, the merchants' havelis celebrated the isolation of the desert with a rich infusion of carving on the exterior facades, and sported paintings inside, screens and fountains to cool the interiors. Most notable among these mansions are the Patwon ki Haveli belonging to five Patwa brothers, Nathmalji ki Haveli and Salim Singh ki Haveli, the former a prime minister of the state and the latter a particularly strong dewan of the state with a penchant for court intrigues. So well did these 19th century havelis emerge that the Maharawal of Jaisalmer had a palace commissioned for himself using the same architectural devices as the havelis. The palace, outside the fort walls, has arches and pavilions and stone screen windows, but in its spread does not have the quality that characterises the havelis.

The royal residences at Kota and Bundi are characterised by the profusion of paintings that embellish the interior. Alwar is known for the slender delicacy of its palaces, specially the City Palace and the later Vinay Mandir Palace; the Italian Renaissance Yeshwant Niwas was abandoned by the Alwar royals as soon as it was commissioned, and a lake fronted palace, the Vijay Mandir commissioned.

The fortifications at Bharatpur were particularly strong, and held the Jat rulers of this desert state in good stead. The Bharatpur royals also commissioned, under defensive fortifications, the pleasure palaces of Deeg, close by. Deeg's *piece de resistance* was the monsoon palace where the royals would relax amidst a plethora of coloured fountains, to the simulated sound of thunder and lightning through an accoustic system devised and built into the roof of the pavilions of the palace. In Bharatpur itself, the turn-of-the-century Golbagh Palace is an excellent example of a harmonious blend of Rajput, Jat, Islamic and British influences in architecture.

A great deal of the furniture for these royal residences was imported from Europe. The royals had a penchant for spending, and they ordered objets d'art rather indiscriminately. Cut-glass furniture was a great favourite. The Jaipur royals favoured Lalique crystal dining and coffee tables, and these are still in use by them. When Umaid Bhawan was being built in Jodhpur its furniture was ordered in England. The ship carrying the first lot was bombed en route to India; a second order was placed, but the factory was burnt down; the Maharaja finally had the furniture copied by his own carpenters.

The royals also built themselves elaborate hunting lodges, for they were fond of shikar; later they were to use these as a means of diplomacy. A particularly good round of hunting with the British viceroy or other colonial administrators often gained them a number of concessions. In essence, the hunting lodges were miniature palaces, and had all the trappings of a royal lifestyle. Rolls Royce cars were available, there was champagne at breakfast, and a few cleverly placed marksmen behind the guests meant a particularly good haul which helped to enliven the atmosphere and keep the guests in a good mood. Alwar was known for its tiger hunts, Jodhpur for its pig-sticking and Bikaner for its imperial sandgrouse shoots.

Apart from palaces, Rajasthan has some beautiful havelis, among them the spectacular painted mansions of the Shekhawati region. These elaborate havelis belonged to traders who controlled interests all over India and in frontier outposts that included what was then Burma. Every surface, be it wall, window arch, ceiling or pillar, was painted. The themes were both religious and secular in content, depending on the artist. There is a prevalence of paintings depicting the Radha-Krishna legend; there are floral motifs; more unusually, there are subjects the artists had never seen but painted from descriptions narrated to them; railway trains, motor-cars, the white sahibs and memsahibs and their alien lifestyles. This also occasionally resulted in some oddities such as the one of the monkey-god, Hanuman driving a Rolls Royce!

The Gaekwads of Gujarat's Kathiawad region administered rich estates and the agricultural prosperity gave them the means to build on a lavish scale. They adorned their palaces with carpets embroidered with threads of gold and woven with pearls and diamonds, indeed, even their cannons were of gold and silver! The traditional residence, the Nazar Bagh residence, gave way in 1890 to the more elaborate Laxmi Vilas palace designed by Major Mant to suit traditional arrangements that called for three distinct sets of apartments : the zenana, the maharaja's chambers and the public areas. Interestingly, the palace borrowed heavily from the Bharatpur fortress, though there were Mughal details in the public rooms, and British style in the billiards rooms and dining rooms and lounges. The palace used bricks, sandstone, marble and blue trapstone. Italian influences crept in, in the form of sculptural adornment and the use of Carrara marble.

Like Jaisalmer, Kutch is a remote place, and as a kingdom it was all but cut off from the mainland, inundated by the sea for practically five months a year. Again, like Jaisalmer, the state's revenues came from trade. Unlike Jaisalmer, much of the Kutchi trade was conducted across the sea. Trade interests established a glass factory, a tile workshop, an iron foundry manufacturing cannons, a workshop for clocks and watches and an enamelling business, all patterned on European usage; the earlier palace at Mandvi too carries European influences: styled on Dutch, Austrian, and Italian sculptural and architectural motifs. It was a folly of a palace, and it cost the treasury more money than it could generate. Internal strife set in soon thereafter, and the British stepped in to administer the state.

Many of Gujarat's royal buildings, be they from Porbandar or Wankaner or Morvi, reveal a strong Italian style, especially in their staircases and their external facades, for seafaring traders carried these influences with them, and they were incorporated with the traditional style. Since there was little similarity between European and other Asian architectural motifs, these buildings represent a style of building that remained restricted to coastal Gujarat.

Along with the forts, the palaces and the havelis, there was a strong tradition of temple building. The royal families had their own deities, and these were honoured in temples, usually placed within the forts. This era also saw a resurgence of Jain temple architecture. This was prevalent over much of Gujarat and Rajasthan, for members of the Jain faith were usually traders by profession. They were also money-lenders, and often bailed the state out of tricky situations. The Jains spent much of their wealth in building a profusion of marble temples with the most intricate sculpture. There were Jain temples in Bikaner and in Jaisalmer; they reached a crescendo in Mount Abu in the form of the Dilwara temples, and were offered the patronage of the Chittaurgarh family under whom the exquisite Ranakpur complex was planned and built. In Palitana, there is an entire hill covered with Jain shrines, a great cathedral to the faith where no visitors are allowed after dark so the gods can slumber undisturbed.

Colour marks the desert in Rajasthan and Gujarat, and therefore it is inconceivable that even the most modest of homes is unadorned. In rare desert outposts, women paint motifs over the entrances to homes; using a mixture of earth and cowdung to plaster the wall and then create designs on the surface. Village women gather to cover an entire wall with a religious wall painting. There is a tradition of continuity, a blend of the aesthetic with the practical. Desert homes, royal or simple, have a splendid sense of presence and belonging to the soil of the land.

*Preceding page: Jaisalmer,
the city of the 'golden fort' is
built of yellow sandstone in
the Thar Desert, Rajasthan. It
is famed for its exquisitely
carved stone screens.
Left: Camels are still an
important form of transport
in the desert near the
fortified city of Jaisalmer.
Above: Desert musicians such
as this one, play haunting
melodies born in the wide
open spaces they inhabit.*

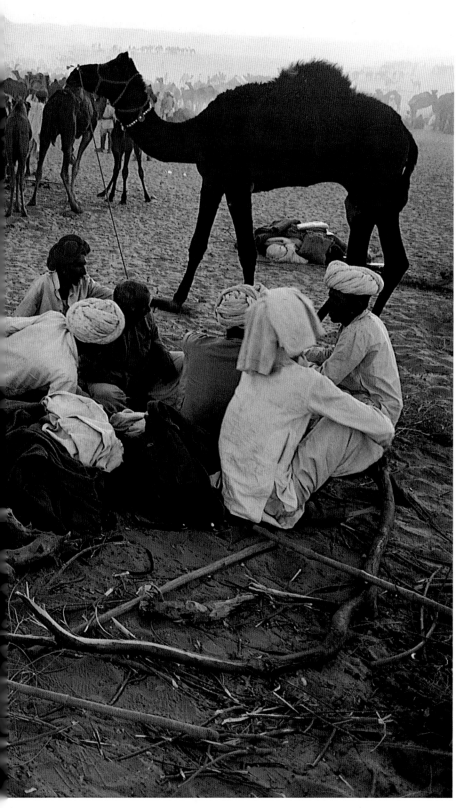

Left: Traders, camelteers and village folk from all over Rajasthan converge on Pushkar for the fair which is held in October or November on a date selected from the lunar calendar. Above: A festively turbanned camel-owner at the fair.

*Above: Exquisitely carved
stone screens are part of
Jaisalmer's traditional
mansions.*
*Right: Folk musicians perform
outside one of Jaisalmer's
exquisitely carved havelis,
built by prosperous
merchants in centuries past.
The desert city once lay on a
major trade route into India.*

Women dressed in their holiday best throng the annual Pushkar Fair, where camels and cattle are brought and sold along with an enormous variety of other merchandise.

Left: The Maharaja of Jaipur performs a religious ritual during the Dussehra festival. Above: The Maharaja with members of his family during the festivities.

हरे कृष्ण हरे राम नारायण सीताराम

In an area of Rajasthan called Shekhavati are unusual havelis or mansions. Every inch of the walls of these havelis is decorated with charmingly whimsical paintings made during the last few centuries.

Above: A royal palanquin in one of the many forts of Rajasthan. Right: Within the rugged Rajasthan forts, are many delicately decorated palaces such as this one, at Junagarh.

*Left: Hunting trophies are to
be found in many royal
Rajput residences.
Above: Artisans in Gujarat
use folk motifs and exuberant
colour combinations to
create fine embroidery.*

Far left: A Rajasthani woman with her cattle, which are a precious source of livelihood in this desert state. Left: A Banni tribal girl outside her mud hut in Kutch, western Gujarat. The Bannis are semi-nomadic pastoralists and are known for their exquisite embroidery.

Left: Cannons on the ramparts of Mehrangarh fort overlook the city of Jodhpur. Above: A royal retainer at one of the palaces within the fort.

Rajasthan's palaces, such as this hall in the palace at Samode, are intricately decorated.

Delhi
The Seven Cities of a Magnificent Capital

NARAYANI GUPTA

Left: Safdarjung's Tomb in New Delhi, built for a nobleman at the end of the Mughal period, is an example of the uninspired architecture of a period of decline. Above: Wrought iron gates form a delicate tracery at sunset, at the President's residence, called Rashtrapati Bhavan.

Every year, birds build their nests on the mossy walls of a very old well near the Qutb Minar. And when the fledglings have flown away, the nests are abandoned. If the story of the 'seven cities of Delhi' is to be believed, so it was with this city. Ruler after ruler built for himself a new capital, each of which was later abandoned. But when I stop to drink a draught of cold water from the old well near the Qutb Minar, or when I walk up to the magnificent Jamali-Kamali mosque nearby, and look out across the landscape of green fields and buildings of dark pink sandstone, as I delight in the dignified beauty and the reassuring strength of old buildings, I wonder . . . Of course there were years and decades when parts of the older towns lay desolate or returned to field and orchard. But field and orchard were then built over, and the town grew again.

Till early in this century, the settlements called Delhi lay in the triangle between the weatherworn, rocky spur called the Ridge, and the Yamuna river. The Ridge has stayed in place, even though much of it has been whittled away by quarrying and building. The river has been changing course, moving further and further east. In the four decades that I have known Delhi, the relentless Lego blocks of an expanding metropolis have covered many stretches of field, meadow and hill. The Ridge used to be ablaze briefly but memorably in spring, with the orange blossoms of the flame-of-the-forest. Today the bougainvillea, exotic to Delhi, has taken over many hillsides and walls in the city, and its exuberant tints, copper-yellow, mauve and red, glow splendidly in the summer heat. Through the year, in ordered sequence, flower the rows of silk-cotton trees (what fun we had as children collecting the cotton pods to stuff our dolls' pillows!), the coral tree (scarlet talons for small hands) and the feathery cassia. As the heat sets in, the variety of fragrant white flowers, frangipani, jasmine, remind one of the days before air-coolers and air-conditioners were used, when we slept on rooftops under the stars, refreshed by the perfume of a hundred flowers. Winter in Delhi is a time of daytime fragrance, the heady pot-pourri of the winter flowers. This gift of the British raj is celebrated in a round of flower-shows, rose-shows and garden festivals, and in the friendly competitiveness between the gardeners of the various parks in New Delhi. And when I stop to buy a bunch of roses from a florist in the crowded shopping-precinct in my neighbourhood I realize how appropriate it is that of all the festivals in Delhi, the one which is unique to the city is the Flower Sellers' Fair in October. For the past century-and-a-half, when the monsoon rains have bathed the trees clean, the flowers-sellers have had a colourful procession of decorated fans blessed at the Hindu temple of Jogmaya and at the Muslim shrine of the saint Bakhtiyar Kaki.

As I water my tiny lawn in the thirsty months of summer, I worry at how much water Delhi must need. And I marvel at the far-sighted rulers who, in the thirteenth century, laid out a vast network of canals here to feed the orchards and the fields which in turn fed the town-dwellers. The canal beds still criss-cross the city and occasionally some place-names, Jorbagh, Motibagh remind me that these neighbourhoods were once baghs or gardens. The precious rain-water of the few months' monsoon was stored in elegantly constructed step-wells, which often had shrines or schools located near them. The river Yamuna has become increasingly attenuated, and Delhi has been built away from it, to the south and the west, but also across it, to the east (locally referred to as 'the trans-Yamuna colonies'). The barriers of the Ridge and the river have been irrevocably crossed by a sprawling city which looks further and further for its supply of water.

The brief twilight in Delhi has for me always been associated with swift flights of homing birds. They dive gracefully into their favourite shelters, very often the eaves or skylights of some ruin. Delhi, like Agra, has been a sandstone-and-marble city. This can be seen in the thirteenth-century Quwwat-ul-Islam mosque, framing the Qutb Minar, and the seventeenth century Red Fort, built by the Mughals to the Secretariat buildings of British New Delhi and the confident buildings of independent India, the architects of which leave their signatures in pink scrawls across the sky. It gives me a great sense of pleasure to come across outcrops of sandstone, serried in horizontal lines, and to know that the natural landscape has not been totally covered by roads and buildings.

They use floodlights at the Qutb Minar nowadays, and this great tower, which has dominated Delhi's skyline for centuries, glows in the dark sky, its slender vertical lines discounting its bulk and strength. When we were children, it used to be possible to scramble up to the top storey. Later, I read a charming account by Emily Metcalfe of how she and a friend used to climb to the top of the Qutb and feast on a basket of oranges, at a safe distance from her stern father, the Delhi Resident. The great carpet of fields, clouded with the gold of mustard blossom in winter, which she and I saw are now overlaid with the grey and cream of flats. Near the Qutb, cocooned in mango-orchards, again for most part now vanished, is the village of Mehrauli, continuously inhabited since at least the twelfth century. Even after the later citadels were built, progressively further to the northeast, Mehrauli was a popular resort in the monsoon season, when the rain filled the air with the perfume of wet earth. Here the Mughal emperors made for themselves a small palace, in the nineteenth century, here Emily's father Thomas Metcalfe converted an old mausoleum for his own use. And here, even now, if one scrabbles in the soil one may chance upon old coins and fragments of pottery.

I have long nursed a wish to be able to locate and traverse all the tunnels said to exist in Delhi. The Tughlaqs in the fourteenth century, the Mughals in the seventeenth and the British in the twentieth are supposed to have constructed these. Dynasties and rulers changed, but all were concerned with security and all were eager to leave permanent mementoes of their impermanent rule. Lal Kot, the citadel near the Qutb was abandoned in the thirteenth century for Siri, built on the flat land further north, and in the next century the palace of Jahanpanah was added. At the same time a massive fort was conjured up within a few years as a post for advance defence. Tughlaqabad today is a crumbling mountain of ruined walls and inner structures, but what a mountain: It is one of the favourite adventure-parks of my children. There is always something new to discover, and the soaring walls, the massive water-storage tank, the skilful use of different levels to create more room are a constant delight for an explorer. Centuries ago, a channel of the Yamuna flowed below the fort walls and a causeway linked it to the mini-fortress in which stands the exquisite sandstone-and-marble mausoleum of the first Tughlaq king.

As I travel on the Ring Road, past Nizamuddin, Purana Quila and Ferozeshah Kotla, I remember that what is road was once river, that it was possible to go by boat from Feroze Tughlaq's palace to the shrine of Nizamuddin, the Sufi saint. Humayun, the second Mughal emperor, a dreamy young man forced unwillingly into the storm and stress of political conflict, built himself an ideal fort along the bank of the river. In this fort, known popularly as 'Purana Quila' (Old Fort) Humayun's little library stands as a memento to this book-lover. Nearby is the mosque built by his rival Sher Shah Suri, which I saw in its full glory when the first rays of the morning sun floodlit its western wall, a sheet of exquisite calligraphy and inlay work. The forts in Delhi have been prey to the weather, to marauders and to neglect. Yet much remains to fire the imagination and delight the eye; one of the most curious sights being that of a great pillar of the Emperor Ashoka (third century B.C.) planted like a flagstaff in Ferozeshah Kotla.

Cities of old had beginnings and ends, boundaries and points of entry. The ruined gateways in Delhi are reminders of caravans of merchandise camped outside the city wall, of people barricading themselves against invading armies, of gates open to welcome festive processions. Now, the context gone, they stand isolated and picturesque; in some cases, only the name survives and the gateways have disappeared. The northern gateway of Sher Shah's Delhi faces the southern one of Shahjahan; the Kashmiri Gate of the latter's city faces the direction of the valley where the Mughals laid out beautiful terraced gardens, Ajmeri Gate the direction of the shrine of Chishti in Ajmer. Gates on the east lead down to the river bank (the ghat, which explains the name 'Rajghat' where stands the memorial to Mahatma Gandhi). Force of habit makes people refer to Shahjahanabad as the 'walled city' though much of the wall has been demolished. The 'walled city', however, is a distinct landscape and a way of life. The city laid out for a small population is now very crowded; in its spacious havelis or houses, inner courtyards have been divided up by people hungry for living-space, its wide avenues have been narrowed by extensions of shop fronts. As my bus ploughs its way northward between Shahjahan's Red Fort and his majestic Jama Masjid, I realize that this road has divided a city which was earlier wholly integrated. Again, when I return to Delhi from Calcutta or Lucknow by train, I realize that the railway line has also sliced the city from west to east in a manner that further destroyed its unity. But as a way of life much that is old still survives tenaciously. The little shops in Dariba Kalan (the Silversmiths' Street) have a charm far greater than that of the glittering jewellery shops in New Delhi. Nai Sarak, lined with bookshops, will in most cases yield the books which New Delhi shops do not have on their shelves. A bride's trousseau can be bought within hours in the shops of Chandni Chowk, which are as comprehensive as any good department store, and a hundred times more lively.

The part of Shahjahanabad which has lost its animation and become a shadow of its former self is the palace-complex, the Red Fort. Behind the massive, beautifully designed wall which separated it from the city lay a mini-town, with halls of audience, offices, workshops, barracks and homes for some thousands of members of the royal family and their attendants. The Peacock Throne of the Emperor inevitably attracted the greed of less opulent rulers, and in the eighteenth century the Fort was repeatedly attacked and looted. But the crisis of the Fort came in 1857 when, for a few months, it was the symbolic rallying-point for a revolt against the British. When the long siege of the city was over, and the British forces regained control, the Fort was occupied by the army. What was more, many of its buildings were demolished, and massive barracks built in their place. Today's visitor, therefore, sees only a fraction of what Shahjahan built.

If the effective rule of the Mughals lasted only two and a half centuries, that of the British was much shorter. But in that time they reduced Delhi from being a capital city to being just another provincial town, complete with railway station, military barracks and civil lines. But it was not easy to exorcise the ghost of Delhi's past. In 1911 when political reasons made it advisable to move the capital from Calcutta, Delhi seemed to be the obvious choice. Over the next twenty years yet more villages in the Delhi District were taken over by the rulers; the villages of Raisina and Jaisinghpura vanished, and a highly symmetrical baroque city was laid out. To me, the building of New Delhi is associated not so much with the rulers, as with the architects. Looking at the centre-piece of New Delhi, at the President's Palace and the two Secretariat blocks, so perfectly laid out on Raisina Hill, nobody would guess that a great partnership lies buried there. The friendship between Edwin Lutyens and Herbert Baker could not survive their numerous disagreements. It was the question of the gradient of the hill that caused the crisis; Lutyens wanted 'his' Palace to be atop the hill, with the Secretariats on the flat ground below; Baker gently moved 'his' Secretariats uphill, and modified the gradient in such a manner that the Palace disappears from view almost completely, for a short distance, as one approaches it. This to Lutyens was *lèse-majesté,* but to us today it is a delightful optical game. New Delhi, the 'winter capital' (in summer the human contents of the Secretariats followed the Viceroy to Simla) is one of the greenest of the world's capitals. Lutyens, like the Indian rulers of old, bordered his roads with tall leafy trees, and embedded each house in its own private garden. There was a strict control on how many people could live in this very formal city, but none on birds. Dusk in New Delhi is memorable for the cacophany not of car-horns but of excited birds. The Lodi Gardens, the most beautiful of New Delhi's parks, was intended to serve the same purpose as a wall would have done in an earlier city — to demarcate the official city from the settlements that would inevitably develop on its fringes. To most of us New Delhi connotes a bureaucratic city, and Old Delhi (Shahjahanabad) a commercial one. For the younger inhabitants, there is another map of Delhi – that of the universities. As New Delhi became inhabited, an older British Delhi faded out from people's memories. This was the Temporary Capital north of the Ridge, which had been used by the officials at the time that New Delhi was being built. To us this is familiar as the campus of Delhi University, and the Vice-Chancellor today receives delegations bearing petitions exactly as the Viceroy used to do earlier. To the south, in the interstices of medieval Delhi, the campus of Jawaharlal Nehru University sprawls athwart the Ridge. Not far from the Yamuna, in the south-east, is Delhi's third university, the Jamia Millia Islamia. The Indian Institute of Technology has a spacious campus on the road from Mehrauli to Ferozeshah Kotla where, in the fourteenth century, there were so many colleges that Delhi was said to have surpassed Baghdad. Near Tughlaqabad is the Jamia Hamdard, a university devoted to promoting research on the history of medicine. Generous areas are set aside for 'institutions' in the planning of Delhi today, and schools and colleges continue to proliferate.

For centuries, Delhi has been 'hazarat Dilli' (sacred Delhi) as well as imperial Delhi. The shrines of the Sufi saints attract a steady traffic of pilgrims. Perhaps the most popular is Hazrat Nizamuddin Auliya, whose name is immortalised in the little township that clusters round his shrine. Redolent with the fragrance of roses and the smell of fresh-baked bread, Nizamuddin is beloved also for the memory of one of the saint's disciples, Amir Khusro, one of Delhi's most popular poets and musicians. Across the road is the mausoleum of a poet and writer of Akbar's reign, Abdur Rahim. When our children recite Rahim's verses in school, or hear the songs of Amir Khusro, all of them do not know that these men lived long ago in this very city.

I am told that Delhi's population swells by some hundreds every day! It is this that changes the landscape constantly, with more and more settlements being built, more and more shops conjured up. Delhi's poets and writers used to articulate a deep love for their city. Do we see an echo of their feelings in the young people who sport T-shirts emblazoned 'I love Delhi'? To a generation in a hurry, who have only a little time to read or to listen to verses being recited, the T-shirt motto is a reminder that this metropolis has so much that can be enjoyed, savoured, returned to; streets reverberating with conversation, quiet places where you can hear birdsong, hotel towers with views almost as spectacular as the one from the top of the Jama Masjid minaret, a modern town through which its hills, its layered sandstone and its river still sparkle out in the most unexpected places.

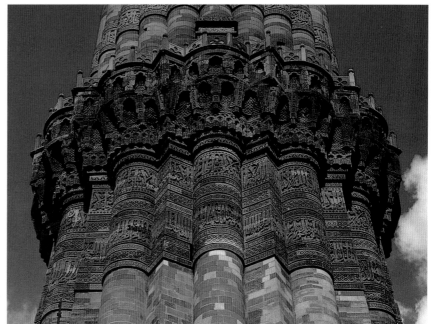

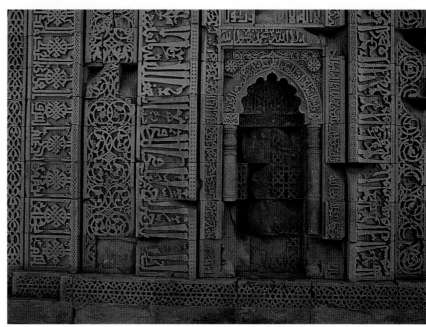

Left: The Qutb Minar, one of the early Islamic monuments in New Delhi, dates back to the twelfth century. Above: It is intricately carved with passages from the holy Koran. Following page: Men gather for Id prayers at the Jama-Masjid in Delhi, built by the Mughal Emperor Shah Jahan.

Above: India Gate symbolises New Delhi, built during the British Raj. Right: Three days after the Republic Day parade, Beating Retreat is held at the foot of the nation's secretariats and Rashtrapati Bhavan. Massed bands of the armed services present a moving programme of martial music, while camels stand motionless against the sky. Following page: Connaught Place is the main commercial area in New Delhi. Modern high-rises are fast overwhelming the low colonial structures of this once gracious area of the city.

The Red Fort, built by the Mughals, faces Chandni Chowk, one of the busiest bazaars in the old city of Delhi.

The Taj Mahal

And the Magnificence of Mughal Agra

SUBHADRA SENGUPTA

Left: The magnificent Taj Mahal, built by a grieving emperor for his beloved wife, has come to be synonymous with India.
Above: Marble inlaid with semi-precious stones, in floral and calligraphic motifs adorns the facade of the Taj Mahal.

For centuries now, it has fascinated us with its elusive, ever-changing beauty. Painters have tried to catch its many moods with brush and pen, in colour and in ink. Writers have struggled to find that ultimate adjective to describe it. Photographers have laid seige to it from every angle of sunlight and by the silvery glow of the moon. None can claim to have captured it completely.

The Taj Mahal.

It is hard to believe that a creation in unwieldy stone can possess such quicksilver moods. That it can take on such ethereal, capricious shapes, making marble change its hues like the ever-moving sea.

Whenever I visit the Taj I wonder at the men who created it. They were builders yes, ambitious dreamers too, and they also understood the magic of theatre. Because the Taj reveals itself with all the drama of a curtain being raised. You enter through a prosaic red sandstone gate and raise your eyes to a fantasy in marble that leaves you transfixed in wonder, as the Taj Mahal once again casts its spell over you. The magic never fails, irrespective of how many times you have fallen prey to the enchantment of its majestic yet oddly delicate beauty.

However, before you visit the Taj Mahal, it is essential to know the story that lies behind it. You cannot go unprepared for such a magnificent show. For it is a unique monument. It was not created in celebration of religious fervour. Nor was it the final symbol of the hubris of a triumphant monarch stamping his name on to the landscape. The Taj Mahal is a monument to love.

A love that an emperor lost. It's beauty comes shadowed by the tragedy of Mughal emperor Shahjahan's greatest love; his wife Arjumand Bano. Married to him in 1612, she became Mumtaz Mahal, the Exalted of the Palace and Mumtazul-Zamani, the Distinguished of the Age. But grand titles could not give her life. Just 18 months after Shahjahan was proclaimed emperor, she died in 1630 at Burhanpur in south India while accompanying him on a military campaign. Arjumand Bano was only thirty-eight.

An emperor's inspiration, a constant companion, a legendary beauty, Mumtaz Mahal's death left Shahjahan devastated. And as a memorial to this great love, he vowed to build her a monument unparalleled in the world. He assuaged his grief through this magnificent dream in marble called the Taj Mahal. 'A teardrop on the cheek of time' in the unforgettable words of the poet Rabindranath Tagore.

It took twenty-two years to build. Skilled craftsmen came from faraway lands, from Persia and Turkey, France and Italy. A site was selected by the bank of the Yamuna River. Then the white grained marble arrived from Makrana, red sandstone from Fatehpur Sikri and yellow marble from the river Narmada.

The plans of the Persian architect Ustad Isa possessed a balance and lucidity that is a marvel even today. For the Taj has that quality which is the hardest to achieve: the elegance of utter simplicity. Not a minaret is superfluous, not a motif or colour is jarring. A red sandstone mosque and its jawab or response frame the marble creation in the centre. Everything blends harmoniously with 'the elegancy, facility and golden cadency' of it as a whole.

Once the marble structure was complete, it was decorated and embellished with the meticulous precision of jewellery. Precious and semi-precious stones were lavished in its exquisite pietra dura work. Tibetan turquoise and agate from Yemen. Ceylonese sapphire, Persian amethyst and Arabian coral. The best jade from China and malachite from Russia. And cornelian, onyx and topaz. Creating a monument majestic in its whole and delicately enchanting in its details. The Taj proves that only the subtle, extravagant Mughals who 'built like Titans and finished like goldsmiths' could create such architectural perfection.

The composition and positioning of the slender minarets, the easy curves of the pointed Mughal arches, the great dome dominating them and reaching to the sky, all combine so skilfully it is hard to believe that the whole structure is 130 feet high. Just the entrance, a soaring archway, inscribed with verses from the Koran in dazzling calligraphy is 90 feet high. Creating an unforgettable amalgam of the opulent symbol of an empire and the contemplative remoteness of a shrine. The loveliness of the Taj always beguiles the mind but I can never forget that it is, finally, a sepulchre.

I have seen the Taj in different seasons in the angled mellow sunlight of winter and in the harsh revealing glare of summer. At dawn, past noon, and by moonlight. It never looks the same. That remarkable marble has the extraordinary capacity to capture the light and reflect a new image in it.

During the day it is massive, glittering white and earthbound. Welcoming you at the end of a row of lily pools and the mosaic garden walk, with a calm majesty. Like a Mughal emperor in court watching you walk up with your small beseeching request.

As the sun dips beyond the Yamuna, the dome and minarets catch the evening's fiery red-gold hue. Moody and moving, reflecting the copper-touched waters of the Yamuna lapping its walls below. On a full moon night, the Taj Mahal floats away from you. Shimmering white against the ink blue sky. A fantasy so delicate and fragile you expect it to vanish like a mirage. And it is hard to believe it is the same Taj you had seen a few hours ago. My favourite Taj is the one you see at dawn, when the gardens are not teeming with people. You sit and watch the horizon turn from the grey of a pigeon's breast to a hazy shell pink. And a welcoming, gentle Taj Mahal turns a serene, rose tinted face towards you. Maybe like the way the beautiful Arjumand Bano once looked at her king.

One day I dream of seeing the Taj from across the river, appearing and disappearing in a winter mist. One day, in a lashing monsoon storm against a slate grey sky. One day. There is always another image that I long to see.

The teeming city of Agra waits outside the gates of the Taj Mahal. The Mughals had an odd affinity to this city. Babur, the founder of the dynasty, missing the cooler climes of his homeland, created a Persian garden here. Then his grandson Akbar, one of the greatest of the Mughals, made Agra the capital of an empire he created by conquest and skilful diplomacy. His son Jahangir, more indolent, though an aesthete of impeccable taste, did little in architecture but left his individual stamp on Indian painting. Finally Shahjahan, the dedicated builder and inspired architect took the architecture of Agra towards a stunning, voluptuous beauty.

Agra has a great deal more to offer the visitor than the the magnificent Taj. Visiting the Mughal buildings scattered across the landscape, you will see a panorama of styles that reflect the age and the monarchs who created them. A fascinating transition from red sandstone to gem-encrusted marble.

Akbar, fighter, strategist, empire builder, chose the robust red sandstone as a building material with which to create with forceful majesty. Jahangir, monarch of a settled empire, was moving towards a more subtle art, introducing inlays and intricate designs but reflecting his contrary character, without any vigour. His son Shahjahan, emperor of one of the richest kingdoms on earth, at the zenith of creativity, chose marble to build with elegant opulence.

I always enjoy the move from the serenity of the Taj Mahal to the grandeur of the Agra Fort. Come down from the heavens and land on earth. Because, going past the Amar Singh Gate, as you enter the Fort you know you are entering the heart of an empire. Three Mughals - Akbar, Jahangir and Shahjahan ruled from this fortress. If the Taj sings of love, the Agra Fort speaks the language of power.

Akbar built the original fort in the shape of a crescent, by the bank of the river, after the walls of an earlier fort called Badalgarh were 'thrown down'. The straight edge runs parallel to the river while the battlements of the curved side face the busy streets of Agra.

The forbidding outer walls, 70 feet high, are the ramparts of a military citadel. Guarded by a deep moat, pierced by slits and loopholes for the archers. But what these walls guard is not an army's barracks but sumptuous palaces and a delectable marble mosque. The contrast between the inner and outer visages of the Agra Fort seem a perfect portrait of the Mughal era. Where might came balanced with civilized, refined sensibilities.

Akbar built it entirely in red sandstone and, for the first time, created an amalgam of Persian and Indian styles. He is said to have filled the fort with over 500 buildings but few of these structures remain. Most of them were demolished by Shahjahan, who replaced them with his favourite marble. Only the outer walls and the Jahangiri Mahal still give an indication of what the fort had originally looked like. The rest is all the grace and taste of Shahjahan.

The ethereal domes of the Moti Masjid are visible above the walls of the Agra Fort. All in marble, its canopies, courtyards and arcaded cloisters hover like a gem over the heavier structures, justifying its serene name, the Pearl Mosque.

The Fort is the place where a busy emperor lived and worked. In the Diwan-i-Am, the Hall of Public Audience and the Diwan-i-Khas, the Hall of Private Audience. Stand a moment by those carved marble pillars and imagine what the rooms were once like. The floor covered with soft, glowing Persian carpets. Tapestries on the wall, chandeliers and mirrored lamps, incense and swaying peacock feather fans. The busy bustle of courtiers and soldiers, ambassadors and slaves. A gorgeous panorama of courtly life in all its pomp and pageantry.

Then, come out on to one of the terraces facing the river. In the distance you'll see the Taj Mahal, a mellow glimmer of marble and again the tragedy of Shahjahan will touch you. At the end of his life he would again face personal grief. Watching helplessly as his four sons began a bloody fraticidal battle for the throne, even though he was still the king. As in all such conflicts, only one son survived – Aurangzeb, who imprisoned his father in Agra Fort and occupied the Peacock Throne. Shahjahan spent his last seven years captive in these marble pavilions of the Khas Mahal. Gazing longingly across the river to the Taj Mahal where he would one day join his beloved Arjumand Bano in the final peace of death.

The Fort is also a place of life and laughter. The Sheesh Mahal, the Palace of Mirrors, is close to the royal apartment and was probably part of the harem. It has hundreds of small mirrors embedded in stucco decorations in floral and geometric designs. Once, slave girls would have carried candles through this room with a hundred dancing flames reflected behind them. A princess' swaying veil would have splashed the walls with emerald and rose-red.

Outside, in the Meena Bazaar, noble ladies played at keeping shop, haggling and flirting with princes of the realm. Or sat among the water courses, fountains and terraces and behind the gossamer lattice work screens of the octagonal pavilion called the Jasmine Tower. Perhaps they enjoyed wandering through a palace intriguingly called Machhi Bhavan, the Palace of Fish, where gaily coloured fish danced through the water channels.

The biggest and most imposing private residence in the Fort is the Jahangiri Mahal, said to have been built by Akbar for his son and heir. In this red sandstone structure that carries the imprint of Akbar's virile style, one can see how he created an unusual mix of Indian and Central Asian motifs, 'in the fine styles of Bengal and Gujarat'. The result is a richly royal palace, elegantly adorned.

Here, stone was carved and shaped as if it was wood. It is evident in the inclined struts in the shape of serpents and the carved brackets under the eaves. The Jahangiri Mahal shows a state of transition from the Hindu palaces to the Mughal style of complex arrangements of apartments to be used by a prince and his entourage.

The Agra Fort, especially the Jahangiri Mahal, sets me thinking of the Mughal who has always fascinated me the most; Akbar. And of his dream city on a hill, the unforgettable, incomparable Fatehpur Sikri. Maybe I am contrary but there are times when Fatehpur Sikri calls to me more than the Taj Mahal does.

Fatehpur Sikri, another offering of Agra that has a story to tell. One with all the ingredients of a fairy tale – a king in need, a boon from a saint, the magical creation of a city by the wave of an imperial hand.

Akbar at twenty-six had become the ruler of a mammoth empire that stretched from the north beyond the Himalayan passes to the deep south of the Deccan. After innumerable battles and alliances, after surviving rebellions and palace coups, the empire was now a stable homogenous whole that acknowledged only one master, Akbar. He had everything a medieval monarch aspired for, undisputed power, great wealth, a harem full of queens. But he had no heir.

In desperation, he visited a hermit sufi saint, Shaikh Salim Chishti in his hilltop retreat by a village called Sikri. Walking barefoot most of the way. The saint's blessings brought him not one but three sons. And in gratitude Akbar decided to create a new capital city at Sikri, in 1569. Only an extravagant Mughal could dream up such a grand gesture, and then make it come true so magnificently.

Fatehpur Sikri. Akbar lived in it for only 16 years. Then, it was inexplicably abandoned and never used again. A ghost city deep-frozen in time. And, because it has not faced the wear and tear of centuries of human habitation, this deserted capital is still in a remarkable state of preservation. As if the passages and palaces are only asleep, waiting through the centuries for another Akbar to bring them alive again.

On a rocky outcrop of sandstone Akbar's new capital city had at its heart the mausoleum of the mystic Shaikh Chishti, set like a jewel in the courtyard of the imperial mosque, the Jami Masjid. Its enormous courtyard can accommodate a congregation of ten thousand and over it looms the immense Buland Darwaza.

If any single symbol of the imperial might of the Mughals is needed, it would be this triumphant, aggressive portal that Akbar built to celebrate his conquest of Gujarat. A gigantic archway, 134 feet high, at the end of a steep flight of steps. And like all such declarations of might it is domineering and impressive but not exciting.

Shaikh Chishti's tomb was later covered in marble by Shahjahan. With intriguingly carved serpentine brackets and marble lattice screens around the porch, that cover the passage around the cenotaph chamber with dappled light and shadow. This tomb gives character to the whole area. Intimate and caring, like the saint who lies asleep within and still gives hope to the millions who visit his sacred grave.

What remains beyond the Chishti tomb complex are a group of palaces used by the royal family. In Fatehpur Sikri in its heyday, a whole city must have sprung up on the lower slopes. Houses of noblemen, markets and workshops. But little beyond the encircling wall and a few desolate structures remain.

The superb palaces of Akbar are located at the end of a steep drive up the hill. This is a city without streets. An asymmetrical grouping of palaces and pavilions, decorative ponds, courtyards, terraces and what were purely administrative buildings, in spite of their graceful styles. Each palace possesses its own individual character in the treatment of architectural motifs but it does not jar because the whole complex is built with the red sandstone of the Sikri ridge itself.

To me, no place brings alive the ages past as movingly as Fatehpur Sikri does. History has been petrified in stone among these palaces and you only need to use your imagination to relive Akbar's time with all its colourful pageantry.

Stand at the central Pachisi Courtyard and it is possible to imagine another day in the reign of Akbar. The terraces thronged with courtiers and noblemen. Sombre Muslim maulvis, dark clad Catholic friars and brahmins in dhotis who followed the emperor from his private chambers to the Diwan-i-Khas for an animated discussion on his eclectic new religion, the Din-i-Ilahi. Or in a lighter vein, on a breezy summer evening with the colourful movement of harem women behind the lattice screens of the five-storeyed Panch Mahal. While Akbar and his friend and courtier Birbal played pachisi with servants standing in as human pieces.

Every palace or pavilion is a different visual treat. Akbar's principal queen Jodh Bai's palace is the kind of home I would have built for myself if I was a princess of the twentieth century. A large paved interior courtyard surrounded by rooms. Private but welcoming, full of elegantly carved walls and delightful maze-like rooms. And on the upper floor one room in which all the walls are finely carved stone screens, where the queen sat to enjoy the fresh breezes. A cool vantage point from where she could watch the comings and goings of the world outside.

Akbar set his own Khwabgah, Palace of Dreams, beside a lily pool. You can stand here and dream of the past again. Because that seat so imaginatively set in the centre of the square pool is where Akbar's favourite singer Mia Tansen sat to perform. Close your eyes and think of a mellow autumn evening, the air redolent with incense and flowers. A gorgeously dressed audience, leaning back against silk bolsters, listening to a raga, as lighted lamps float in the water.

Akbar's imagination has an unexpectedness which did not always produce elegance but it did create edifices of truly startling design. Take his Diwan-i-Khas, the Hall of Private Audience. It looks like a double storeyed building from the outside but is actually a high ceilinged chamber with an extraordinary pillar set in the centre with passages radiating from it on the top. It is said Akbar sat on the top of the heavy pillar with the courtiers standing around the circular gallery around the four bridges. It is not elegant. Shahjahan would never have permitted such a creation. But you never forget it either.

There are many visual delights in Fatehpur Sikri. The structure they now call Birbal's palace but which was probably part of the harem, with its profusely decorated exterior. The astrologer's seat and behind it the pavilion which guides will fancifully tell you was the room where the king played hide 'n' seek with the harem women but which was, more prosaically, the royal treasury.

Akbar chose not to be buried at Fatehpur Sikri but at Sikandra, near Agra. He began the construction during his lifetime but it was completed during the reign of his son Jahangir. In its slightly confused design, an ungainly mix of sandstone kiosks and fragile canopies topped by a latticed pavilion, Sikandra marks the transition between the Akbari and Shahjahani styles.

The Jahangir era produced one gem of architecture that should not be missed. The tomb of Nurjahan's father Itimad-ud-Daulah. Jahangir's queen, Nurjahan was more than the empress, she was the real power behind the throne. And she lavished her legendary good taste to create a perfectly proportioned marble building set among geometrically designed gardens. Exquisitely decorated with mosaic and inlay, it is the forerunner of the Taj Mahal. Being built entirely in marble, it uses pietra dura inlays with lyrical subtlety.

Before leaving Agra every visitor ought to wander a bit around its maze-like lanes. In many ways, the city retains an almost medieval character in the leaning houses and dim shops full of unexpected treasures. For the craftsmen of Agra have much to offer. Intricate marble inlay work in Mughal designs and velvet purses and shoes embroidered in gold in the traditional zardozi style. Agra's cuisine is both rich and subtle and still carries a flavour of those lost days of imperial splendour.

I always leave Agra with my mind a whirl of images and experiences. And I always know I'll come back again. There's so much more to see. The Taj in the rains, Fatehpur Sikri by moonlight, a quawwali recital on the sun-warmed stone before Shaikh Chishti's tomb . . . Agra will beckon and I will return.

Emperor Shah Jahan, who built the Taj Mahal, was imprisoned in the Agra Fort at the end of his life. It is said he drew comfort from this view of his wife's tomb across the curve of the river. Following page: The river Yamuna flows behind the Taj Mahal. In Mughal times, the Emperor frequently travelled by boat to the Taj.

The Taj Mahal is set in a geometrically precise formal garden, which is believed to symbolise paradise.

Facing page: A Buddhist monk at the entrance to the cenotaph chamber of the Taj Mahal. The arched doorway is decorated with finely carved marble screens and inlay work. Left: Details of the fine stonework at the Taj. Above: The dome is surmounted by a lotus and finial in gold leaf.

*Left: Inside the Taj Mahal —
Mumtaz Mahal's cenotaph is
in the centre, under the dome
and Shah Jahan's to the left.
They are enclosed by a
delicately carved marble
screen. Above: Detail of the
calligraphy inlay on the royal
cenotaphs.*

Above: The Agra Fort, beside the river Yamuna, is built of red sandstone. Right: The many-pillared Hall of Public Audience in the Agra Fort. This building, like many others inside the fort, were built by Shah Jahan, although the fort itself was built by his grandfather Akbar.

126

Left: Part of the magnificent palace complex at Fatehpur Sikri, the city built by Emperor Akbar outside Agra. Above: The tomb of Sufi saint Salim Chishti at the mosque in Fatehpur Sikri. Top: The structures at Fatehpur Sikri are built of red sandstone, quarried from the ridge upon which it is located. Following page: The lyrically lovely Taj Mahal, built of pure white marble, is flanked by a mosque on one side and a rest-house on the other, built of red sandstone.

Central India

Forests, Palaces and Tribal Settlements

BILL AITKEN

Left: A cow which predicts the future and a seller of hats at a village fair held on the occasion of Maha Shivaratri near Bhopal. Above: A finely carved image of a god.

Wherever I have gone in Central India, the same sense of being near the heart of the Indian experience has marked my travels. The first time I crossed it meaningfully, from south to north, was on a trip by local bus from Bangalore to Delhi. I was so fed up at missing out on the local culture between these two cities that I vowed to linger in the Deccan and make my way home slowly, savouring those delights the long distance train sweeps by.

That journey took me five days and was immensely enjoyable. Ask me what I remember most about it and odd, inconsequential details pop up, such as the sound of home-made lime-soda bottles being uncorked (with vintage marbles in their neck), and the remarkable cultural unity of the straggling Deccan plateau, shown in the similar design of sari worn by women as far apart as Bellary and Gwalior. Above all, it was the friendly, relaxed pace of the local lifestyle that appealed. Even in the central Indian cities there is little of the frenetic seething that marks the usual urban turmoil of north and south.

The country bus was slow, its crew invariably affectionate and its casual approach to distant goals a tonic after grim tourist itineraries. Transport anywhere outside 'Middle India' takes on the fixed Euclidian urge to traverse quickly between two points as mindlessly as possible. Such journeys by their tension (and series of narrow squeaks) leave the passenger exhausted, for the human soul was not designed to travel much faster than a government chaprassi on a bicycle. For this reason I view the state of Madhya Pradesh not just as the heart but the soul of India.

It is a kindly province for sure. Never in my travels here have I been rudely spoken to, nor had my plans been ruffled by irrational ire. Perhaps because of its physical size and the reassuring sense of space, the citizens of central India do not feel threatened by strangers. Its blank spaces on the map always appeal to the dedicated traveller and the little-visited areas of Madhya Pradesh must be among the most inviting in India. It is annoying not to be able to pin down exactly the appeal of this gentle rambling state but at least any search to define its elusive charm will arouse the pleasure of memorable days savouring nature at its freshest.

Madhya Pradesh's mild elixir next hit me when I did a narrow gauge train journey from Chandrapur (in Maharashtra) to Jabalpur. Known as the Satpura lines, this railway system was opened at the start of the century to tap the bamboo wealth of central India. As it happens, the Satpura railways add up to the world's largest narrow gauge system and when I visited the area, steam power was still hauling the trains. In another railway record the daily Satpura Express left Jabalpur each morning at five and thrashed its way to Gondia, 225 kilometres south. Then in the afternoon, it returned to Jabalpur before midnight, the world's oldest regular narrow gauge steam Express, till diesel took over in recent years.

We left Chanda Fort in an ancient carriage whose underframe dated back to 1909. Not surprisingly, few speed records were set by that groaning train. It dived straight into thick bamboo jungle and brushed a way through the boondocks. The progression of unspoilt rural scenery as the tough little engine overcame the Satpura gradients included the typical sun-dappled broad-leafed teak clearings of middle India. We didn't get to Gondia till quite late but had the pleasure of watching the sun set over the Wainganga, one of the south-flowing rivers of Madhya Pradesh.

I didn't go all the way to Jabalpur by train that time but hopped off at the small junction of Nainpur. Here I caught an old German steam engine that tottered over a branch line to the centre of Gond tribal culture at Mandla. I had been impressed by the ruined fort at Mandla where the lovely Narmada sweeps round to create a place of tribal pilgrimage. The Gonds had the distinction of being the last of the native opposition to the Mughals.

From Mandla, with its fascinating tribal museum, I struck out west to follow the Narmada to its source. Most visitors to this friendly town turn the other way towards Kanha National Park, considered to be the amongst the best managed in the subcontinent. I took an ordinary passenger bus of Madhya Pradesh Roadways which ambled along without any urgency and allowed me to see the colourful tribal lifestyle at the series of tea halts along the course of this ravishing blue river. I was struck by the devotion of the pinched villagers who, whenever the bus had to ford the stream, would offer a tiny coin from the folds of their garments. This spontaneous affection for the river goddess came across as a much more profound gesture than the theatrical associations that surround the sacred (and commercialised) waters of the Ganga in the northern plains.

As the sole passenger on the bus late at night I could only sense the closing in of the forest from the flicker of the headlights. At the pilgrim mini-township of Amarkantak there were no lights and everyone had apparently gone to bed. It took me an hour to grope my way to a government tourist bungalow and it was not until next morning that the chowkidar explained that the village had not been asleep but packed into a thatched hut to see the latest video film. I woke to a scintillating cool breeze of the leafy, salubrious Maikala Plateau where the tiny ribbon of the holy Narmada set off on her long journey west to the Arabian Sea. Some soaring temple spires stood against the skyline, obviously inspired by the Khajuraho school but these had no erotic details. The plateau overlooked a dramatic void where amidst the lush cover of the dense growth of teak the infant Sone river hurled herself into space north-eastwards to ultimately join the Bay of Bengal. Within the space of a few feet rose two rivers that measured the whole width of central India. So ecstatic was the geography of this riverine conjunction that one could easily understand why the British had been forced to erect railings to safeguard the pilgrims. In the old days, properly initiated persons, who were suffering from an incurable disease or who had committed a particularly heinous offence, would offer themselves to the gods by leaping off from this magical void in an act of ritual suicide.

Drunk with the beauty of Amarkantak, my next trip was to approach it from the tribal tracts of Orissa. This meant climbing up from the coastal town of Kakinada in Andhra Pradesh in a laborious crossing of the Eastern Ghats to Koraput. Again one had reached a rolling plateau fresh in its cool delight. Later the bus passed through the lost forests of Dandakaranya, cleared to house the refugees of the 1947 Partition of India. By evening the forest had again taken over and one arrived in Jagdalpur, the capital of the tribal Bastar region. As innocent as the tribals, I went around the small town shooting away with my camera. It was not until I was back in Delhi that a professional photographer informed me that in these tribal areas it was illegal to take photographs without permission.

I would have liked to linger in Bastar to see its waterfalls and wildlife but time and funds were running out. In one day and night I travelled the entire length of Madhya Pradesh, about 1000 kilometres. At Jagdalpur I caught a so-called luxury bus to Raipur and then transferred to a State Roadways vehicle that went via Amarkantak to Rewa, near my ultimate destination, Khajuraho. That marathon journey had me looking longingly out of the window at some of the ranges of dense jungle we traversed which beckoned loudly for a return visit. Ravishing rock formations, stunning stands of trees, mesmerising rivers; these are some of the features of Madhya Pradesh that always pull you back.

Having fallen head over heels in love with the Narmada I now planned a circuit that would include both river and tourist sites, and another interesting destination that rumour had fuelled. I caught the overnight Malwa Express train from Delhi and next morning alighted at Vidisha to see the ancient remains of Buddhist and Hindu empires. While in other states, Buddhism has been savagely treated by the mainstream religion, in Madhya Pradesh the virtue of tolerance is still to be seen in the excellent state of preservation of Sanchi. This lack of fanaticism makes Madhya Pradesh an ideal state to visit in an age where in both north and south, regional culture has begun to trumpet its superiority. Central India has no need to assert an aggressive identity since it combines the best of both.

What is most inviting to the visitor are the well run tourist bungalows dotted around the state. Their architecture is invariably delightful and in their modest profile (and tariff) may be found echoed one of the secrets of this unsung region's appeal. It is the home of Kalidas, the outstanding poet of India's Sanskritic past. Life-affirming graces seem to come naturally to the most rustic of one's companions along the way in Madhya Pradesh.

I had been told about a supposed stone-age community which lived in a deep canyon in the tribal belt and whose contact with civilization was limited by the inaccessible valley they inhabited. After scouring the physiographic map I concluded this story was a leg-pull but determined nevertheless to try and find out what had sparked off the legend. The first place I asked was at the bus station in Bhopal and pat came the immediate answer. The name of the village was Patalkot and it lay near Parasia, a coal-mining area served by the friendly narrow gauge Satpura lines.

The bus across the Satpura was a delicious ride through Sal forests. It remains in the memory for the happy sight of the conductor sitting all the way up front with his arm around the driver's neck. Next day on another bus out of Chindwara the crew was similarly disposed to entertain the passengers, only this time instead of Mills and Boon romantic interludes we were treated to Laurel and Hardy slapstick. The conductor had a walking stick he used to prod the driver when the bus laboured up inclines. Another use of this stick was for the driver to flash it out of the window to clear a way through herds of cattle blocking the road.

From the map I had deduced that Patalkot would have to be in the Mahadeo range. Some black contours indicated the prospect of beetling cliffs and my guess was it this impression of depth that had given rise to the legend of a beleaguered tribe. The scenic road from Chindwara to Pachmarhi climaxes in the village of Tamia and there in the tremendous fall of cliff and jungle lay the ingredients for the hidden-tribe myth. I hired a bike and cycled for 15 km along the brink of the Mahadeo range astonished to find a level road tailor-made for tourists. Then the great rift appeared and land dropped away in awesome crags that cascaded an impressive stepped progression down to the distant valley floor, altogether in exhilarating scene. Puzzled by the spruced up notice board announcing Patalkot and a brand new flight of steps that set off vertically over the lip of the void, I spoke to a tribal. He was the village headman who had come to welcome a group of visitors. When he said he had been waiting since nine in the morning (it was now two in the afternoon) I guessed the group he referred to must be on government duty. Patalkot is now very much on the map.

That night I spent at the Tamia dak bungalow, one of the most spectacularly sited resthouses anywhere outside the Himalayas. All around the cliffs fall away in yawning drops and the march of unbroken forests in the distant valley make this a sumptous study in dramatic landscapes. Looking north, I was shown Dhupgarh, the highest peak in the Satpuras rising above the thickly forested ridge that concealed my next destination, the small hill station of Pachmarhi.

It was in this tidy and beautifully sylvan little town that I came across the clue to the stone age reference in the Patalkot legend. Pachmarhi must be the only place on earth where there is a potential black market in prehistoric paintings. Madhya Pradesh is comparatively rich in rock and cave paintings and the precipitous terrain on which the hill station of Pachmarhi has been founded probably means that some paintings have yet to see the light of day. Without question this is the best preserved of all Indian hill stations in terms of natural beauty and in maintaining the British ethos of a quiet retreat. The bazaar was tiny, with hardly a newspaper to be had. The only distraction was the pom-pom of brass bands going through drilled rehearsals, for Pachmarhi boasts of an academy of military music.

The wooded walks, cliffs and waterfalls made this a splendid place for nature study while the hard but pock-marked black lava of the mountain sides gave perfect finger and toe holds for the rock climber. All around lay the lush jungle that India was once famous for. Kipling would have been happy to know that at least one corner has been saved for the creatures of his *Jungle Book*. (His Seoni lies south-east of Pachmarhi).

From Pachmarhi, I descended to Hoshangabad to follow the Narmada to the sea. Thirty years earlier, while still a student at Leeds University, I had corresponded with a Gandhian worker at Rasulia near Hoshangabad. That was the time of the Bhoodan movement and our student support group had contributed towards the cost of a well for his village. Later, I had gone to the village and met the social worker. More than anything else, it was the way he had conducted the Gandhian prayers in his house that stood out. I sensed that the grace visible in his person had been inspired by the beautiful mood of the river flowing nearby, the gentle Narmada.

Twenty years later I found the mood of Hoshangabad hadn't changed. I stopped at a shop in the bazaar to ask where I could buy some typing paper and whether there was a place where I could hire a bicycle to ride down to the stepped bathing ghats of the river. The shopkeeper, who sold cloth, insisted I come inside and sit down. He offered me tea and said he would give me paper from his own stock. We drank the sweet tea in small cups (though the locals prefer to drink it from the saucer) while a small boy was sent to the bicycle hire shop to bring me my vehicle, for which the shopkeeper offered to stand guarantee. You meet with these spontaneous gestures of kindness all the time in these central provinces. It might be noted that the kindness is never (as in other parts) followed by an exchange of addresses or any suggestion of a quid pro quo. You are a visitor and in the culture along the Narmada the guest is God. It is probably this genuine expression of traditional Indian hospitality that hits the traveller most. Elsewhere, it has either been watered down or gone commercial. My own theory is that being so spaced out the area lacks the press of competitive bodies. There is no threat to the rustic rhythm of life. The stranger in one's midst therefore is not a person to fear but someone to be enjoyed, and welcomed.

Most of the year the river at Hoshangabad is broad and blue and to follow it down to the border of Gujarat is to experience the Narmada at her loveliest. Pilgrims toil along the banks, and temples mark their halting places. The golden ghats at Maheshwar announce the handsome seat of the great devotee Queen Ahilyabai but the past glories of religion fade before the grim evidence of drought in the fields that the great river bypasses. Lower in the gorge at Mandhata, the sacred islands of Omkareshwar stand out as a craggy seat of pilgrimage amidst the ageless flow.

Near Jabalpur, on my first narrow gauge journey, I had gone to see the Bheraghat marble cliffs on the Narmada. The journey was performed in a three-wheeler taxi which announced it could carry 10 passengers. On board were at least 30 bodies jammed in so tight that each time somebody got out you could hear the vacuum pop. The cliffs, viewed from a rowing boat, were tiresomely touristy but the escape to the magnificently secluded Chausath Yogini temple (above the Dhuadhar waterfalls) was an exquisite bounty. The circular display of richly sculpted goddesses took one's breath away; such exultant beauty in stone verged on the miraculous.

By contrast the ancient temple at Omkareshwar is one of the twelve Jyotirling temples, the embodiment of Lord Shiva. It was here that the great reformer-philosopher Adi Shankaracharya received his initiation as a boy. While Bheraghat yields the white marble from which many of Hinduism's household gods are fashioned, the george at Mandhata provides the large, egg-shaped green polished lingams sacred to Shiva.

On my first traverse of the Deccan I had made a point to visit Mandu, whose superb Islamic ruins overlook the distant Narmada in the middle reaches of the river. The sheer style of this early Muslim capital make it an outstanding architectural experience. Bold, original buildings combine strength with harmony. Mandu is like a Brahms symphony in stone. Sadly, on a recent visit, I discovered a crude attempt to 'Brahmanise' the place. This bizarre falsification of the evidence shows that not even Madhya Pradesh can escape the unfortunate trend to edit history according to the needs of the party in power.

A visit to the nearby towns of Dhar and Ujjain turned out to be stimulating and rewarding. Typical of small town Madhya Pradesh they both have civic character and neither display that tragic air of municipal collapse that characterises so many towns along the Ganga.

While on a motorcycle tour of the Chambal river I side-tracked to have a look at the small town of Datia. What magnificent architecture awaited us in this tiny town with its upraised Palace (Govind Mandir) in the centre. It bowled me over as no other building has done. Next day, by chance, while driving west to Shivpuri from Jhansi I happened to see a signpost that pointed down a lane to Survayu Fort. Inside was the most lyrically beautiful little temple I have ever set eyes on. Thus on one casual trip into Madhya Pradesh I was transported twice to rare regions of pleasure by some astoundingly lovely buildings. Middle India to a traveller is what an old book shop is to a scholar. You never know what to expect next and the tingle of discovery forever enlivens your itinerary.

If I have left Khajuraho to the end it is not because one needs sex to keep the narrative on Madhya Pradesh from flagging. In point of fact the sexual details of Khajuraho's resoundingly beautiful temples are irrelevant to their glory, the physical exuberance is a sideshow to the sheer spiritual aspiration on view. The temples must count amongst the world's most chaste architectural expression.

My introduction was at the end of a numbing day and night journey by bus and it was with apprehension I approached them for the moment of truth. Would they be like the Taj Mahal, a trifle overrated, where geometrical satisfaction has been confused with solace to the spirit ?

I held my breath, lifted my head and as the sensational outlines of the temples floated before my vision I realised the lesson central India had been trying to teach me. The finest in the human spirit always responds to nature at her freshest.

At Jabalpur in Central India, the Narmada river tumbles over marble cliffs on its journey to the ocean.

Prehistoric cave paintings at Bimbetka, near Bhopal, reach out across the centuries with their vitality and expressive dynamism.

The beautiful Gwalior Fort is an interesting example of Hindu architecture in the early 16th century.

A folk dance in a tribal area of Madhya Pradesh follows the rythmic beat of a pair of drums. It is performed during the festivities that mark the harvest season.

Left: Tribal folk dances are still an intrinsic part of life in remote areas. Above: A folk dancer.

Panels of sculpture from the exquisite temples at Khajuraho. Each figure seems almost alive, so skillfully have they been sculpted.

Above: The complex of palaces at Mandu, near Bhopal is especially beautiful during the monsoon. Right: At Orchcha, near the city of Jhansi, are structures built by the medieval Bundeli kings. One palace has been converted into a hotel, enabling visitors to stay within the walled complex.

Left: Buddhist monks excavated caves across the face of a ridge at Ajanta and decorated them with exquisite murals about two thousand years ago. Above: Sculptures from the Hindu and Buddhist caves at Ellora near Ajanta.

Madhya Pradesh has several beautiful wild life sanctuaries which harbour a substantial tiger population.

The Fabled Coast

HUGH and COLLEEN GANTZER

Left: Stunted trees struggle to survive on the edges of the salt marshes on the west coast. Above: Coconuts ripening on the tree in Trichur, Kerala. This part of the west coast is famed for its abundant coconut groves.

At midday, the mirages began to form. They shimmered at the edge of the salt-encrusted plain, shifting on the sun-bleached horizon. Out of the unreality, reality emerged, took form, began to thunder towards us on iron hooves, cracking the surface of the cement-hard sand. On they came, closer and still closer, twenty magnificent wild asses at a gallop, muscles rippling under their fawn-and-chestnut coats. Suddenly, they spotted us and, as swift as a flight of wild geese, they wheeled about and vanished into the mirage again.

We were standing in the Rann of Kutch. To our left, curtained by the illusion of green trees reflected in a lake which wasn't there, was the imaginary line in the salt wastes dividing Pakistan from India. Behind us, the breakers of the Arabian Sea rolled in. This was the start of the fabled, 7516.5 kilometre coast of India.

Great cultural influences have surged in through the coasts of India, into this sub-continental land, creating that complex matrix out of which India has evolved, and sustained itself, as the world's oldest continuous civilization. Embedded in this matrix is the cult of a dark-visaged pastoral god-king named Krishna. He had his legendary capital in the coastal town of Dwarka. When we drove from the Rann to Dwarka, cows ambled down the narrow streets. We attended a ceremony in the great Dwarkadhish temple at which the idol of Lord Krishna was being dressed in royal garments. Then the curtain of the sanctum was drawn and, while bare-chested priests chanted and clanged cymbals, a worshipful congregation greeted their Lord.

Obeying Lord Krishna's command, the sea once retreated to allow him to build his city, and then it returned when he died. Legend? Possibly. But marine archaeologists have found evidence of a city lying submerged beneath the waves off the mainland town of Dwarka and the island of Bet Dwarka where Lord Krishna is said to have had his palace.

We left Dwarka behind us, travelling south in a bus crowded with fisher-folk and redolent of the sea. Giant wind-farms paddled their power-generating arms before we reached Porbandar. Here, the home of Mohandas Karamchand Gandhi has retained its simplicity. But a great palace-like establishment has grown up in front of it. "Why do you have such a resplendent facade to such a humble dwelling?" we asked one of the officials of the Gandhi Library. "Because," he said, "the most precious relics must be displayed in magnificent settings!"

Further down the coast, a decrepit old Ambassador taxi dropped us at the entrance of the summer palace of the former Nawab of Junagadh. Chorwad palace, as it is called sits elegantly on the beach. It is grey and pensive, like a European stately home. Now a state-run hotel, it is frequented by conventioneers, honeymooners and affluent families escaping from the urban carousel. In a guest-mix unheard of ten years ago, hand-holding honeymooners shared the palace hotel with a convention of celibate Catholic nuns and priests discussing the future of education in India. "What did you see, Sister?" we asked a nun as she and six of her colleagues alighted from a tourist coach.

"Somnath," she said cheerily.

The three priests and four nuns, all dressed in their habits, had visited one of the holiest shrines of Hinduism without giving it a second thought. 'Hinduism,' according to the *Encyclopaedia Britannica*, was a term invented by English writers in the 1830s to describe 'an utterly diverse conglomerate of doctrines, cults and ways of life.' Thus, catholicism and tolerance is the very essence of Hinduism: a fact which political fundamentalists of all types find very difficult to admit.

Consequently, when the proselytising Portuguese sailed into India in the late 15th century, the absorbing faiths of India disturbed them. It is difficult to convert a person who believes in the equality of all religions. The Portuguese stayed on, for four and a half centuries, colonizing a part of the west coast and their influence lingers in the architecture and lifestyle of this region.

South of Chorwad, at the beach retreat of Ahmedpur-Mandvi, we sat in a brightly painted tumbril mounted on a powerful motorcycle, which roared across a causeway to a Portuguese-built city on the island of Diu. A statue of the first Portuguese governor, Nino da Cunha, stood proudly in a frowning fort: cannon thrust their noses from the battlements: and Father Mario said Mass to his congregation in Portuguese. A widow in rustling black said softly: "My nationality is Indian, my culture is Portuguese. Nationality is the blood; culture is the way you live."

But not all foreign influences survived on this coast. The first British trading post, or factory, was set up in the teeming coastal town of Surat around AD 1612. Here, too, came the Armenians and the Dutch. We picked our way through weed-covered rubble to a ruined building in which early British traders had reputedly once lived. And then we wandered silently among the headstones of the British and Armenian cemeteries. A slim young man, whom we mistook for a gardener, came up to us and asked, "Are you the buyers from Amsterdam?" Surat is one of the leading diamond cutting and polishing centres in the world and our questioner was, probably, one of the three hundred thousand diamond workers of Surat, who bring out the lustre in these glittering stones.

We swept down the coast in an air-conditioned coach, diverted to pause at a place called Sanjan. To Sanjan, thirteen hundred years ago, came Zoroastrians from Iran fleeing persecution in their homeland. The local king sent them a bowl filled to the brim with milk to indicate that his kingdom had no room for the refugees. The Zoroastrians, however, poured sugar into the brimming bowl without spilling a drop of milk. They were permitted to stay on and their descendants, called Parsis today, are a thriving, self-reliant community who still maintain their ancient faith.

Today, the principal town of the Parsis is Bombay, the commercial capital of India. Traffic became chaotic as we got closer and closer to Bombay. Once part of the Portuguese colonies, it was given to England as part of the dowry when Charles II married Catherine of Braganza. The area was developed by the British till it grew into a megalopolis which many foreigners regard as the most international city in India: a description disputed by many other cities.

The beaches of this commercial hub are at one end of what could well become the Gold Coast of India: a long, southern-stretching, band of tourist-enticing beaches. Boarding an Indian Airlines flight we winged our way over the gold, silver and black-gold strands of coastal villages, towns and territories saturated with history. And as we flew high above them, tales of the fabled coast kept rising like genies released from old bottles washed up by the surf.

There were places such as Kihim and Alibagh, associated with piracy and ship-wreck and battles between British men-o'-war and swift local fleets. We had spent a weekend on Kihim's beach, discovered its tiled cottages with hibiscus in their gardens, followed creaking bullock carts down shady lanes, discovered an old Portuguese fort some distance away and wondered when the forest would cover it once more, reclaiming it for its own.

And there, visible from the air, was mysterious Murud-Janjira, with its forbidding sea fort skirted with surf. We remembered our visit to the lonely island fortress and how we sailed across the bay in a flimsy fishing boat. In the fort, darting swifts had arrowed chevrons across still, green ponds; a wind-driven window had gone *creak-thud! creak thud!,* and there was the fragrant smoke of a cooking fire where none should have been. Later, we were told that an old man and his mad, young wife lived in this lonely, sea-washed fort. But she was happy in her madness because she sang and cooked for him and wanted no other world but that scrub-tangled fortress on a lonely island in the sea.

Our flight skimmed in low over Goa's palms and cashew trees, and the sea glinted sapphire-blue beyond. We collected our luggage, walked out of the airport, and flagged down two 'Pilots': motor-cycle taxis licensed to carry a passenger each. It was a wind-whipped drive along roads laid down by the Portuguese during their four hundred and fifty year rule here. We passed wayside shrines, old white churches and red tiled cottages where old people sat contentedly on rocking chairs. The relaxed, Mediterranean-like atmosphere of Goa, the fact that many of the local people wear western dress and have a fairly western lifestyle, and the magnificence of its beaches have made Goa a prime tourist destination.

On the ferry between the capital, Panaji, and the bus station on the other side, we spoke to bearded, bright-eyed Francis Cardozo, who looked like a Professor of Oriental Languages but claimed to be 'a commercial agent dealing in all sorts of things'. We asked him if he thought that the influx of tourists would destroy Goa's unique Indo-Iberian culture. "No way . . ." he drawled. And then he cast a weather-eye on two young Europeans of indeterminate sex and dressed in well-patched and not-too-clean motley. "Maybe we can teach them something about culture!" he said, and laughed.

We caught a bus, crossed in another ferry, and accepted a lift in a Japanese-designed, Indian-made Maruti van owned by S. Balakrishnan Nair. The saturnine, quick-witted Nair had the compelling good looks of a handsome Mephistopheles. He had joined the Gulf exodus of people from the state of Kerala, made his fortune in one of the oil-rich kingdoms, and was now back home seeking a good investment for his money. During the 714- kilometre drive to Cochin in Kerala, Nair regaled us with snippets of the state's history, unaware that we had spent nineteen years here. "This is the real spice and coconut coast," said Nair. "But it is more. Do you know that

Christ's apostle Thomas came here in AD 52? You know that? Good!"

In 1498, Portuguese navigator, Vasco da Gama landed south of Cannanore near the port of Calicut. He made contact with the local king, the Zamorin, and took back seedlings of the pepper vine. Descendants of these plants, established in the former Portuguese colony of Brazil, are the strongest competitors of Indian pepper in the world's spice markets.

A little before we got to Cochin, Nair pointed to the right. "Down that road is the ancient port of Cranganore, once known as Muziris, now called Kodungalore. There is a temple to the Mother Goddess there and the correct offering to make to that temple is pepper. So it is a great pepper collection depot. That is why the Romans, Greeks, Phoenicians, Arabs, Jews . . . everyone . . . came here. Then a number of floods silted the river and opened the estuary at Cochin." He did not, however, mention the fact that the first church on the subcontinent as well as the first mosque were established in Cranganore. These were already thriving places of worship before the Portuguese came to Cochin.

Cochin explodes and grows on both sides of an estuary: its twin city of Ernakulam, fairly modern, on the right bank; the older settlement of Cochin on the left, dating back to the days of Vasco da Gama. Seaport, airport, railhead and business heart of the state of Kerala, these grown-together cities are a ferment of aggressive politics, devout traditions, hard-headed commerce and green palms and silver waterways winding through the most unexpected places.

The waters of the estuary flow down from many sources, including the area called the Kuttanad. Alleppey, down the coast, is the gateway to the Kuttanad and here, on the second Saturday of August every year, they hold the world's largest team sport: the Nehru Trophy Boat Race featuring war boats, each one rowed by 100 oarsmen. Rowing down the coast in a war boat might have been a great adventure, but we preferred to hire a cab and drive down to the bottom of the V of India. Our driver, Raju, fancied emblazoned T-shirts ('Next to my skin I like you best') and fusion music: a soothing amalgam of western pop and Indian classical. He told us he was a follower of Narayana Guru, a contemporary of Mahatma Gandhi. The guru had broken the priestly monopoly of the Brahmins, established his own temples, and proclaimed a faith of 'One caste, one religion and one God for mankind'. "He established a major centre in this town, Varkala," our driver said, showing us red cliffs rising out of a small beach. "Healing mineral waters flow out of those cliffs," Raju assured us.

And then, later, as he drove us into our hotel on Kovalam's scimitar-sweep of black-gold sand, Raju advised: "If you look carefully, sometimes you might see a rocket in the sky. Very near is the Thumba Equatorial Rocket Launching Station from where we put weather satellites into the sky, I think so. Is a great thing, no?" We agreed that it was, and walked down for a bath in the warmest, gentlest sea we've ever experienced.

The sea at Kovalam had unravelled the travel kinks from us when we left the greenness of Kerala behind us the next morning, and headed for the Land's End of India: Kanyakumari. Here, the Arabian Sea, the Indian Ocean and the Bay of Bengal meet, and the shore temple of the Virgin Goddess gazes at the island temple to a modern seer, Swami Vivekananda. In front of the memorial dedicated to Mahatma

Gandhi we met a widow who had renounced the world. We asked her why she had chosen to spend her years here. "You know the tale?" she asked. "Here, the Virgin Goddess was tricked out of her husband by a mischievous seer. That is why the sand here is shaped and coloured like the rice, lentils and charcoal left over from her ill-fated marriage feast." She looked up at us and smiled with great serenity. "She was deprived of a husband, so was I. She understands me."

When dawn rose over the three seas, we left Kanyakumari and began to ascend the eastern coast. The Bay of Bengal now lay on our right and we stopped at the shore temple of the warrior god Murugan: he had defeated submarine demons here, in Tiruchendur. We drank water at a pool created by the thrust of Murugan's lance, within spray distance of the sea. Then we drove on to Rameshwaram.

The island of Rameshwaram, linked to the mainland by a bridge, has a sprawling temple famed throughout India. It commemorates the legendary victory of a northern Prince, Lord Ram, over the southern king, Ravan of Sri Lanka. It was here that we saw a devotee of Ganesh touch his forehead, his left and right shoulders, his heart and then join his hands. When we asked him what he was doing, he said, "I'm offering the Lord the strength of my mind, my shoulders, my heart and asking him to accept them." To us it looked as if he was crossing himself the way Catholics do.

The Bay of Bengal had begun to get rough and white horses were tossing their manes on the sea when we came to the quaint town of Pondicherry. This was a French colony for centuries. French is still spoken here, the police wear kepis and many of the activities revolve around the Aurobindo Ashram: an international community dedicated to finding alternative lifestyles to today's consumer-oriented civilization. In many ways Pondicherry's fortunes have been linked, down the centuries, with the cultural and commercial magnetism of the historic port of Madras, a little further up the coast. Here, Robert Clive laid the foundations of the British Empire and Madras still has a regal, slightly colonial air about it. When we pointed to the statues of British generals and monarchs which still adorn Madras traffic islands, and asked why they hadn't been removed as has been done in northern India, we got an illuminating reply. Said shopkeeper P.K.K. Muthu: "Their civilization is hardly a thousand years old. Our culture goes back before Egypt. Why should we be scared of western imports. In fact, we welcome them!"

Driving out to Madras' suburban beaches in Mahabalipuram we saw great rock-cut temples, bas reliefs and an ancient lighthouse. From here, the Principal of the local Sculptors' Academy informed us, Indian seafarers spread Indian traditions to Indonesia and south-east Asia.

We had to hurry on because black clouds were rolling across the sky and it was raining fat drops when we reached the crafts town of Machilipatnam. This old coastal town is noted for the beauty of its block printed fabrics and the fury of its storms. "We are near a geo-magnetic anomaly . . . whatever that means . . ." administrator Krishna Rao told us. "In the last storm people saw flames leaping out of the sea and a huge wave rushed in like a monstrous mountain of water."

We continued our journey northwards. A storm warning had been hoisted for some hours before we reached Visakhapatnam. This burgeoning city claims to be the fastest growing port in Asia but it might escape the grime and over-crowding that industrial growth often brings in its wake. Local laws demand that every new factory create and maintain its own verdant setting: casuarina groves promise to make the twenty-four kilometre road from Visakhapatnam to the former Dutch settlement of Bhimunipatnam, one of the greenest beach stretches in India.

The clouds were being shredded by the wind and there were patches of blue in the sky when we drove out of Visakhapatnam. We were no more than half-way up the east coast and the hinterland was becoming more benign, dotted with farms and green fields. The tower of the much-revered temple of Lord Jagannath rose above the palms. Originally a tribal, totemic deity, Lord Jagannath, his sister Subhadra and his brother Balabhadra were absorbed into Hinduism. Every year thousands of devotees drag the enormous wooden chariots of these gods in Puri so that the deities may leave the confines of their temple and go to another temple for a brief vacation. The movement of the giant chariots is so difficult to control that they have given the word 'juggernaut' to the English language.

The wind off the sea sursurrated through beach forests of casuarina as the town of Lord Jagannath fell behind us and the Sun Temple of Konark grew ahead. Buried under shifting dunes of sand for generations, this 13th century temple is now an archaeological monument and on the World Heritage List. It represents the chariot of the Sun God pulled by spirited horses.

The Bay of Bengal was a sheet of dimpled glass as we left Konark and headed for the increasingly lush lands of West Bengal. Flooded fields of jute flashed like mirrors in the dark soil. Then the coastal dunes began. In the rather simple beach resort of Digha, old women in white collected shells washed into the burrows of fiddler crabs, and sold them to the shell workers who crafted them into a fascinating array of figurines of gods, goddesses, and the most delicate animals.

Then, the road plunged into a wilderness and the coast of India curved east and spread into a network of distributaries. These are the delta lands of the Sunderbans, the 'Beautiful Forests'. We boarded a flat-bottom boat and put-putted along the creeks and backwaters which India shares with its neighbour, Bangladesh. Dense, swampy, mangrove forests slid by. Somewhere inside these swampy jungles prowled the massive Royal Bengal Tigers. Tribes of honey collectors also squelched through these dark and misty forests. They wore masks on the backs of their heads to ward off man-eaters. We spoke to a honey collector. "Do your masks frighten the tigers?" we asked.

He shrugged. "How do we know what the tiger feels?" he replied. "All we can do is to believe what out ancestors believed. Such traditions protect us."

He then paddled away in his skiff and vanished into the river mist. We thought of the mirages in the Rann at the start of our long coastal odyssey. In all ancient civilizations, reality grows out of unreality, and illusions have a strange, self-sustaining logic that defies time.

Fishermen in Kerala building a boat known as a 'catamaran' which literally means logs of wood tied together. Following page: Fishermen go out to sea at dawn in their insubstantial looking craft.

Left: Fisherfolk pull in their nets on the coast of Goa. Above: An informal fish market springs up on the sand as the catch comes in.

Left: The body of St. Francis Xavier, said to be miraculously incorruptible, lies in a gilded casket in the Basilica of Bom Jesus in Goa. Above: A thanksgiving procession at harvest-time in Goa.

Left: The famed shore temple
is one of many beautifully
sculpted monuments at
Mahabalipuram near
Madras. Above: The Gateway
of India at Bombay was built
during the British period, to
commemorate the visit of the
Prince of Wales.

Exqusitely carved temples at Konark on the east coast are still the objects of pilgrimage to the devout. Following page: Sunrise at Kanniyakumari, the southern-most tip of the Indian sub-continent, where three seas meet.

The South
Where all Faiths Meet

S. MUTHIAH

Left: One of the many temples of South India, where a tradition of stone sculpture has created some beautiful places of worship.
Above: A painting in the Tanjore style from south India, depicting the god Krishna as a small child.

India's tranquil South is a historic land of tradition and ancient custom. Here, where Nature's bounty flowers in infinite variety, the faithful count their blessings in year-round festivals of invocation and thanksgiving, celebrated at the shrines of all faiths. Nowhere in India are the marks of tradition, the practices of custom and the faith that's an intrinsic part of both, a more vivid, vibrant and visible presence in the fabric of everyday life than in the South.

On the southern reaches of the legendary Coromandel Coast, where the sacred river Kaveri spreads out and creates a verdant delta, there are three little townships that symbolise Southern beliefs. A short drive from each other, a morning's walk apart; are Thirunallar, near Karaikal, once-French enclave that's a part of Pondicherry, Nagore and Velanganni. Pilgrims worship Lord Siva in Thirunallar at the best-known temple to Saturn in India, wash their sins and ills away in the tank of the gleaming Nagore mosque and seek the blessings of the Virgin Mother and beseech Her for miraculous cures beneath the tall steeples of the church in Velanganni. Truly are people of all faiths one here and truly have the gods blessed them for this oneness. For behind this stretch of coast, washed by the waters of the Bay, stretches the ancient land of the Cholas and the Pandyas where the crops flourished and art and culture spread beyond the seas to the islands of the east and the lands of the Menam and the Mekong.

Here are Thanjavur and Tiruchchirappalli and Madurai, ancient cities when India was young. This is the heartland of the Tamil people, whose language and culture go back two thousand five hundred years and more. And here were born and reborn the Tamil language, Carnatic music, Bharatha Natyam, that most ancient of all classical dance forms, and sculpture and architecture that in their exquisite beauty are a paean to the gods.

On the banks of the sacred Kaveri is Thirvarur where not one, but the three great pillars of Carnatic Music were born. And in nearby Thiruvaiyyaru, every January, the greatest exponents of Carnatic music gather to pay spontaneous tribute to the Trinity in a festival of music that combines worship and music in a way that is unique.

Echoes of this music are heard in the sculptured corridors and beneath the *gopurams* that tower over the portals of the temples of the heartland. There can be no village without a temple, the ancients decreed. But in this part of Tamil Nadu, the temple-builders have surpassed themselves in creating shrines that remain a joy for ever. In Madurai, ancient capital of the Pandyas and home of the sangams that created the literature of the Tamils, the magnificent temple of the Goddess Meenakshi is fit to rank with the wonders of the world. Four magnificent *gopurams* or spires soar over its portals, a thousand-pillared hall enthralls and evokes visions of past splendour and everywhere there is sculpture, ornate here, pristine there, exquisite wherever man has put chisel to stone.

The artisans of the ancient land of the Tamils were the greatest stone sculptors of them all. And some of their finest work survives in and around Thanjavur. The grandest temple in all India is how the Brihadeeswarar Temple in Thanjavur has been described. And its grandest feature is its soaring gopuram, towering not over an entrance, as is the convention, but over the sanctum itself. What the all-conquering ruler wrought in the 11th century, his son threatened to surpass in Gangaikonda-cholapuram after he had made all India his, to the banks of the Ganga. But in the end, filial respect made him build a gopuram a mite shorter, but nothing could stop him building a more beautiful temple.

Temple art and Carnatic music are not all that the Kaveri delta has nourished. It was in the temples they built that the Chola rulers encouraged the handmaidens of the gods to dance to their Lords. And, here, to the rhythm of slapping feet and tinkling anklets there was born again the dance the ancients had written a code for, Bharatha Natyam, the most classical of all Indian dance forms. It was to take a few hundred years more before Bharatha Natyam was to move from the temples to the stage and become a more universal art form, but in those days when dance and worship went together, it was the temples of Thanjavur that nourished the revival. Appropriately, every posture of the dance has been sculpted on the pillars of the awe-inspiring temple to the Lord of the Dance, Lord Nataraja, in Chidambaram.

Besides song and dance, every delta town also nurtured a spectacular range of crafts. From weaving silks to making exquisite jewellery, from embellishing paintings with gold and silver leaf to creating rare beauty out of bell metal, craftsmen wrought exquisite materials out of fabric and stone, metal and wood. These skills have not been forsaken even in an age where the land of the Tamils is among the foremost industrialised regions of a nation racing to catch up with the 21st century.

Three centuries earlier in the region around Madras the Pallava kings were laying the foundations for the flowering of Chola art. From their great ports of Mylapore and Mamallapuram, their ships sailed to the lands of the east. In Kanchipuram, their capital, they built temples worthy of one of the most sacred cities in India and everywhere, they encouraged the weaving of the finest silk in all India. The temples of Kanchi, the open-air museum of exquisitely sculpted living rock in Mamallapuram that's still a feast to the eye after weathering the sands and winds of centuries, and the ghosts of ancient Mylapore where the peacocks once danced and the sixty three saints sang, are every bit as enchanting as the riches of the land of the Cholas.

In the land of the Pallavas and in Chola Nadu are two historic cities whose stories are the links between ancient Indian glory and the India of today and tomorrow Mylapore was a thousand years old and more when Madras was founded on a surf-wracked spit of no man's sand by an English factor looking for a place to get "cloath better cheape". And it was from the fortified warehouse he established here and called Fort St. George that there was to grow an empire on which the sun did not set for nearly 200 years.

Forty years after Madras had sunk roots, a French soldier established a little bit of France in Chola Nadu and called it Pondicherry. And seventy years later, Francois Dupleix and his Begum Jeanne dreamt of an empire the like of which the world had never seen. For over twenty years thereafter, the French and the British battled in the plains of the Carnatic, between Madras and the ancient land of the Cholas, and when the British won, the dreams of Dupleix had become theirs.

In Madras and Pondicherry are the remains of those dreams, as much symbols of an empire on which the sun set as memorials to what it contributed in its zenith to the greater glory of modern India. In the Indo-Saracenic architecture of Madras, in the Regency style of Pondicherry and Madras are the first vestiges of the splendours of Calcutta and Bombay and the vision Lutyens created in Delhi. Wander through the corridors of Madras and you wander with the ghosts who laid the foundation of much that we take for granted in the India of today: governance, military traditions, education, engineering, medicine, you name it, much of it was pioneered here.

South of the rich plains of the Carnatic are the parched southern plains of Tamil Nadu that reach to the end of India. Towering out of arid, scrub-covered landscape are the mansions of Chettinad, built by former merchant princes who made their fortunes from Sri Lanka to Vietnam and used their wealth to embellish the temples of Tamil Nadu, revive the glory of Tamil and build those homes where hospitality was unlimited.

Beyond Chettinad are the temples and the towering steeples of the churches of the legendary Fisheries Coast whose pearls were sought throughout the ancient world. On the sacred shore of Pamban island, is Rameswaram, sanctified by Lord Rama offering thanksgiving to Lord Siva here for making victory possible over the demon king Ravana. And here the Ramanathaswamy Temple has been built as a fitting symbol to such piety. One of the most magnificent temples in Tamil Nadu, it is famed for its spectacular corridors, over 1200 metres long, every foot of the way testament to the skills of the sculptors of this region.

Further south, overlooking the bay where they once dived for pearls and where they still dive for sponge and seaweed and coral, are the churches Francis Xavier inspired. Amidst them is the beautiful temple to Lord Muruga in Tiruchendur, one of the six abodes to the Lord in Tamil Nadu that ought to be visited in turn to complete life's long pilgrimage. And then there's Land's End.

Land's End is a sibilant whisper of travel romance befitting an area of great beauty. Here, where three seas meet and seven sands mingle in beaches that are riot of colour; here, where you can watch the sun set and the moon rise from the same spot, religion and faith permeate the very air. The temple to the Virgin Goddess Kanniyakumari, the shrine built to the Father of the Nation, Mahatma Gandhi and the memorial on the rock rising from the seas, upon which Swami Vivekananda sat and meditated before taking the gospel of Hinduism to the West are also the end of the pilgrim's progress that began in the shrines of the cold Himalaya, passed through Varanasi and Ujjain and reached journey's end here.

Moving westwards from Land's End, up along the Malabar coast, it is in Padmanabhapuram, with its wood and tile-roofed shrine and palace of the Maharajahs of Travancore, that the varied landscape of Tamil Nadu meets the lush green of Kerala, a sliver of land shaped like the segment of an orange. From earliest times its ports have provided a haven to Arab and Chinese traders who made entrepots of them. It was in search of the riches of these trading ports that there came the Jews and the ocean voyagers of Portugal and Holland, Britain and France.

In the roofs of home and palace and temple and in the mechanical fishing nets of Cochin and other ports there remain memories of China. Near Cranganore is where Christ's disciple, Doubting Thomas, landed, and in seven pilgrim centres are the churches that have grown around the shrines he built. Near where Thomas Dydimus landed is where the Arabs brought the first words of the Prophet and built the first mosque in India, pre-dating the Mughal contribution by centuries. And from Cranganore to Cochin, the Jews established their settlements, finding sanctuary that both Sephardic and Seraphic could not find in the lands they called home. The synagogue the White Jews built in Cochin, and where a miniscule congregation still worships, with its Chinese tiles and golden scrolls must be one of the most beautiful in the entire Jewish World. Home to all, Kerala offered its hospitality to all faiths. Yet nowhere in India are Hindu festivals more fervent, more tradition-bound yet more spectacular than in the shrines at Guruvayoor and Trichur, Trivandrum and Sabarimala, where bare-bodied worhsippers are a stark contrast to gaily caparisoned elephants on the march.

Kerala, the land of the coconut, is a fertile land between high, forest-clad mountains and blue seas that wash golden beaches. Between mountain and sea are fast-flowing rivers, calm backwaters and a blessedly fertile soil. Its waterways make travel possible by boat from north to south. And when there's a temple festival beside the backwaters, the snakeboats are launched again and to war cries of the past the men of today churn the waters and race their long boats.

This racing tradition is one of many traditions associated with art and action. The Kathakali is another, in which dancers weave passionate dramas as they dance. In this and other dance traditions, forms have been preserved and transmitted from one generation to another, by dedicated and skilled gurus. There is also the ancient ritual of Kalaripayattu.

The Western Ghats, that long, high mountain ridge that cuts off the richness of the narrow plains from the rest of India, are perhaps the most beautiful part of Kerala. Here the trees grow taller and the forests thicker as rain and mist and mountain cool nurture both plant and animal. And where the forest has been cleared, beauty of another sort carpets the mountainside, in the emerald of the tea bush. Forests where the elephant and the deer, the tiger and the Indian bison called the gaur, the Indian ibex that's the Nilgiri Tahr and the leopard all roam. And here, where man and animal live side by side in peace, three states meet. Here too, Kerala, Karnataka and Tamil Nadu have some of the finest national parks and game sanctuaries, in Wynaad and Eravikulam, Bandipur, Mudumalai and Anamallai. And near them are the finest hill resorts in all South India, Ooty that is the 'Queen of Hill Stations' and where they still ride to the hounds, Coonoor and Kotagiri surrounded by the tea bush, and not far away, gentle Kodai, where a search for the stars in the skies is as much a part of life as walks through woods and by precipice's edge.

It's a world apart from the fishing villages and rice farms of Kerala and the village variety of Tamil Nadu made a unity by the towering *gopurams* in each. The year-round cool in the hills is as much an experience in India's south as being soaked by the monsoon in Kerala or being burnt by the sun on the plains of Tamil Nadu.

North of the sanctuaries at the tri-junction is royal Mysore, beyond which are the splendours of Karnataka. Regal Mysore, curious amalgam of sprawling palaces in

Indo-Saracenic style that are today museums, hotels and homes, public buildings and official residences. Here silks and sandalwood products in all their variety are part of those riches of development, but perhaps richest of all are the Brindavan Gardens a few miles northwest where dam-building skills have been crowned with a beautiful garden of flowers, lawns, lights and fountains. But none of this built beauty compares with the human surge that makes the Dassara festivities every September-October a ten-day riot of procession, colour and gaiety. The city becomes a fairyland of lights, the daily processions are dominated by caparisoned elephants and exhibitions offer all the fun of the fair. And, for those ten days, once former royalty finds a place in the sun again.

East of Mysore, Srirangapattanam, on the banks of the sacred Kaveri, recalls those glorious days when Tippu Sultan took on the might of three British armies and died defending the breach in the walls of his fort and capital. Here, midst beautiful lawns, he and his kin lie buried and on the walls of his summer palace are told the tales of his deeds of derring-do in colourful frescoes.

West of Mysore are the forested ghats, sloping steeply down to the rice plains of the west and the golden beaches of the Konkan Coast beyond, nourished by monsoon rains, gushing rivers and spectacular waterfalls. Here is Kerala repeated in many ways, except that on the slopes of the Ghats tea doesn't carpet the clearings; this is India's coffee country where the berries ripen red and bless many a Coorgi family with not only an outdoor life but also prosperity. When the Coorgis are not planting, they serve the nation in its armed forces, continuing a martial tradition that is as much reflected in their folk dances as in their wedding celebrations.

North of Mysore is where the ancient sculptor and builder made rock beautiful and embellished the glorious traditions of the Tamil stone-workers. In Halebid and Belur and Somnathpur the Hoysalas built temples whose exquisite sculpture is sheer poetry. From the lace-like effects of Halebid to the epic carvings and polished pillars of Belur and the magnificent sculpture of Somnathpur, this is another part of Karnataka where the skills of artists make mere mortals marvel at what Man is capable of. In nearby Sravanabelagola stands a 58-foot statue of the Jain Saint Gomateswara – and its simple beauty is a sharp contrast to the ornate embellishments in the Hindu shrines of this region. In every sculptor's stroke here there is a serenity that reflects the austerity of the Jain faith.

Further north there is more history and beauty in stone. In Badami, are cave temples hewn with great artistic skill, in Aivalli the beginnings of South India's Dravidian temple architecture are seen in the oldest temple of the south, dating back to A.D. 450, in Pattadakhal the northern Nagara temple architecture has grown by the side of southern Dravidian, all three locations together lessons in stone to students seeking the story of the development of temple architecture in a land of temples.

In nearby Bijapur, the Adil Shahi dynasty of Muslim rulers have left behind buildings of great beauty, none more so than the Gol Gumbaz with the world's second largest dome. And in Hampi are the remains of the greatest empire of the South, Vijayanagar, which once ruled all of peninsular India from the palaces and temples now seen here in ruins and restored splendour.

From Hampi, the journey south takes the traveller to the garden city of Bangalore, capital of Karnataka. Once a sleepy British cantonment town whose parks and gardens were its greatest attractions, it is today India's fastest growing city. But the parks and gardens remain as much a part of it as pubs, billiard halls, shops and restaurants whose food has made eating out a part of life.

From Bangalore, heading east past the country's only major gold mines near Kolar, is Tirupathi in Andhra Pradesh, the country's richest temple. Sprawled over the top of one of seven hills are splendid facilities for the thousands who flock to the hill-top shrine, seeking the blessings of Lord Venkateswara.

Not on the pilgrim route but a place which should be visited is Nagarjunasagar, where a giant man-made lake has submerged all of ancient Nagarjunakonda, the greatest seat of Buddhist learning in the South. However, before much of the waters were let in, most of the treasures of Nagarjunkonda were saved and relocated in an island museum which reveals, as much as nearby Amaravathi does, the Buddhist influence in South India centuries ago, when even sacred Kanchi was a major centre of Buddhist learning.

North of the wild country that's the Srisailam sanctuary near Nagarjunasagar is Hyderabad, capital of Andhra Pradesh but once seat of the Nizams, rulers possessed of fabulous wealth. Everywhere in Hyderabad there's a palace to see, a mosque to admire and rich Hyderabadi cuisine to enjoy. Near the most renowned of Hyderabad's landmarks, the Charminar, are the bangle-sellers, the pearl market and the perfume makers who team to attract every visitor to the city as much as its fabulous Salar Jang museum, where one man's collection of bric-à-brac never seems to be exhausted, to judge by the constantly announced changes of display.

To the west of Hyderabad is fabled Golconda, whose diamonds the world coveted for centuries till the South African finds. In a spectacular fort sprawled over several hills there is architectural splendour worthy of the great dynasty, the Qutb Shahis, who founded Hyderabad 400 years ago. Today, Golconda is a ghost town, where, on a moonlit night's picnic, the soft music and tinkling anklets of court performers are a ghostly presence or so visitors say.

Further north, Andhra offers wild country again. Warangal, centre of Andhra's 'lake district' was the seat of the Kakatiya rulers. Sculpture abounds in temple, palace and fort, the temples of Hanamkonda and Ramappa the most splendid of the lot. East are the magnificent gorges of the Bison Range, the beautiful rugged Araku Valley and the Borra Caves rich in stalagmites and stalactites. Here is Nature at its most wonderful and its most bountiful till you reach the coast. And there, the northern Coromandel has even more splendid beaches than the southern Coromandel. Exploring those beaches and moving south is to first reach Vishakapatnam, where the Navy and the ship-building industry dominate the town, and then Madras, once 'Gateway to India', now, for many years 'Gateway to the South', a land of temples and tradition, culture and natural beauty, a land of great serenity and greater hospitality.

A devotee prostrates himself before an image of a hooded Cobra, guarding the entrance of the snake temple at Nagarcoil. Following page: A panoramic view of a temple complex.

At Mahabalipuram outside Madras are several beautiful rock carved temples and bas-reliefs. The most magnificent of them all is this rock sculpture, in which a natural fissure in the rock has been used to portray the descent of the Ganga to earth, surrounded by celestial beings and rejoicing animals.

Facing page: The entrance to the main temple at Halebid in Karnataka, is flanked by finely sculpted images depicting kings and queens, gods and goddesses, celestial beings and animals. Left: An intricately carved pillar inside a temple in Belur, near Halebid. Above: the Nandi Bull, Lord Shiva's vehicle outside the Virupaksha temple in Pattadakhal in Karnataka.

187

*Facing page: A priest in a temple dedicated to Lord Vishnu. The mark on his forehead symbolises Vishnu.
Left: Priests gather at an auspicious hour outside a temple as they wait for the doors to open for ritual worship.*

Kuchipudi dancers Raja and Radha Reddy are exponents of a dance form from Karnataka.

*Above left: In Kathakali, the female roles are also danced by men.
Above: Kathakali, the ancient dance-drama of Kerala is still a vibrantly
living art form. Dancers wear mask-like make-up, made of rice flour
and colour. Right: Tayyam is a folk dance from Kerala in which
dancers wear elaborate make-up and head-dresses.*

The Maharaja of Mysore sits in state under the royal umbrella during an annual festival. Facing page, top: Wrestlers greet the Maharaja before commencing on a match. Below: Silver and gold carriages await the Maharaja of Mysore and his family outside the royal palace.

Left: The Mylapore temple in Madras is ornately decorated with images of gods and goddesses. Right: The impressive hall of worship at the Madurai temple in Tamil Nadu. Following page: The main entrance to the Meenakshi Temple of Madurai is through a colonnade of shops; the walls are lavishly decorated with figures of gods and goddesses.

Buddhist India

The Path of the Buddha

RENUKA N. KHANDEKAR

Left: A sculpted head depicting the Buddha at Ratnagiri. Above: An image of the Buddha at Leh monastery, Ladakh.

My mother had been a dancer in her youth, and growing up, I learnt religion through body language – the ten avatars of Vishnu that seemed a curious parallel to the theory of evolution; (the ninth was the Buddha). I learnt of Navarasa or nine basic emotions drawn upon by actors and dancers, of which the ultimate, Shanta (Peace) was depicted by a Buddha-like meditational 'lotus pose'. All these, plus a fund of myth, legend and folklore were taught as stories, replete with gesture, movement and spirit.

Nature too was often explained in terms of religious belief – the sacred tulsi housed the spirit of Vishnu, the holy peepal (*Ficus religiosa indica*) was the Bo Tree under which the Buddha found enlightenment and the full moon of Baisakhi was also Buddha Poornima because his birth, enlightenment and death all occurred on a Baisakhi and made the day especially holy.

The Buddha was born in the 6th century BC to King Suddhodana, a chieftain of the Gautama clan of the Sakya tribe. He ruled at Kapilavastu with his queen Mayadevi. Before her son's birth, she dreamt that a white elephant from heaven circled her thrice and entered her womb.

The court sages interpreted this to mean that a son would be born to her who would be either a great king or a spiritual leader.

As is still the custom in India, Queen Mayadevi set off to give birth at her parents' home which was in the foothills of the Himalayas. On the way, her cavalcade halted at the beautiful Lumbini gardens. The queen stepped out to admire a blooming Ashoka tree and as she held its branches, the Buddha was miraculously born from her right side. The mystery was compounded by the presence of heavenly beings and by the fact that the newborn, wrapped in finest Varanasi silk, took seven steps, each placed on a lotus that sprang from the earth to receive his foot.

The queen returned to Kapilavastu and while the kingdom rejoiced, the baby was prophetically named Siddhartha, signifying goodness and true understanding.

When the prince was still a little boy, a sage called Asita came to the Sakya court and prophesied that Siddhartha would become not a Chakravartin (emperor) but a Buddha (an enlightened being).

His father, King Suddhodana did not approve. He wanted his son to be a great ruler, and weld the Sakya clans into a great force. He took care to surround the boy with every conceivable luxury and reared him carefully within the palace and its grounds, screened from the ordinary lives of people outside.

Siddhartha studied the scriptures, learnt riding, archery and music and all the skills and graces a royal prince was expected to have. To crown his happiness, he was married to Yashodara, the lovely, accomplished daughter of a Sakya nobleman,

Dandapani, whom he won in a traditional swayamvara or tourney of potential bridegrooms. He stood the triple trial of prowess in archery, wrestling and intelligence (the sacred river said to be released when he shot his arrow was the quest of Kipling's lama in *Kim*, arguably the finest fictional portrait of a Buddhist monk and human being ever drawn).

But though Yashodara proved a loving wife and a son, Rahul, was born to them, Siddhartha was somehow detached from all the pleasures that surrounded him and tended to go off into bouts of deep thought that alarmed his watchful father.

One day, the prince went for a ride with his charioteer Chandaka, and saw an old man hobbling past. Kindhearted Siddhartha stopped and asked Chandaka what ailed the old one. His answer, that it was merely the inevitable decay of age that befell everyone, was a rude shock to the prince.

Nor did two subsequent discoveries, again on drives outside the gilded palace help: it was not old age, but sickness and death that lay in store for all beings. The final blow was the sight of a monk, a sanyasi, who had renounced all earthly bonds, passing calmly by with a begging bowl.

Siddhartha stole away into the night, abandoning his sleeping son and wife, cut off his long, princely locks and exchanged his royal silks for the coarse cotton worn by a chance-met hunter. His life as Siddhartha was over.

For months on end, the wandering prince went from one renowned teacher to another across the eastern Gangetic plain. He was honoured as a seeker by the Magadhan King Bimbisara at Rajagriha, but went on to study nearby with the seven hundred disciples of the sage Ramaputra Rudrantaka.

The fasting and rigorous mortification of the flesh advised by the sage as sure keys to wisdom did not seem quite right. Siddhartha took courteous leave and went to Gaya, along with five other disciples. They stayed at a place called Gayashirsha Hill, celebrated in Hindu myth as the spot where the demon, Gaya, had been thurst into the earth. The band of six seekers moved on again, to a village called Uruvilva by the banks of the river Nairanjana. The Sakyamuni (holy man of the Sakyas) as Siddhartha was now called, began to question the validity of physical penance as a means to salvation. Disappointed, the other five went away to a deer park in Sarnath, near the city of Varanasi.

Sakyamuni sat alone in the padmasana (lotus pose), straight-backed, legs crossed and folded, arms down, in the yogic posture for meditation. He stilled his thoughts and looked inwards, eating only a single sesame seed a day.

For six years he sat starving and thinking till he became positively skeletal. There are haunting sculptures from Gandhara, now in Afghanistan, of the fasting Buddha, that are incredibly moving and make you wonder what went through the mind of Sujata, the little village girl from Uruvilva when she offered Sakyamuni the rice pudding with which he broke his terrible fast.

After that futile exercise, Sakyamuni took to wandering again, but only along the peaceful river Nairanjana. He decided to try meditation one more time and chose a leafy peepal to sit under, having begged some grass for a seat from a friendly grasscutter called Swastika. Circling the peepal seven times, he sat again in the padmasana, facing east towards the sun, the source of life and light.

But before the light came darkness: Mara, the king of evil, sensed the potential threat of goodness and tried to break Sakyamuni's meditation with the lures of his daughters and the threats of his sons. But the seeker held fast and touched Mother Earth with his hand, invoking her protection. Mara finally had to admit defeat.

And then it happened..A great light washed over the Buddha's whole being and he understood, at last, the Cause of all things. He was now the Buddha – the Enlightened One.

The Buddha rose from his seat of enlightenment and he travelled north along the Ganga to the deer park at Sarnath, near Varanasi, in search of the five disciples who had left. When they saw him, his shining face made them fall quiet and listen.

This sermon, the Dharmachakra Pravartana (which set in motion the wheel of law) has been painted on frescoes, carved on rock and stone, while Sarnath with its deer endures even today.

What the Buddha said on that memorable day is still the living core of Buddhism. It is aptly called the Middle Way. The Four Noble Truths are:

All Existence involves suffering.

Existence itself is illusory and ephemeral.

The cause of suffering is thus the desire for illusory things, sensual and material wants.

Suffering will end only when Desire is snuffed out.

His method of controlling Desire was outlined in the Noble Eightfold Path.

Right Speech, Right Action, Right Livelihood, Right Training, Right Awareness and Right Concentration, which lead to Right Meditation and finally to Nirvana, Enlightenment.

The Middle Path swerved not a hair – it rejected both extremes of asceticism and self-indulgence. Though its goal was Moksha (deliverance from the cycle of birth and death) it was not, as many wrongly believe, a negative creed.

In fact it defined a meaningful span on earth as one that did right by one's fellow beings and urged the deepest sort of happiness – the kind found only in selfless service, in *not* allowing anger, jealousy, lust and all the dark forces in human nature the upper hand. Nor, unlike deferral religions that promised rewards in the hereafter, did it let an individual skip responsibility *here* on earth.

It's easy to understand why the five disciples sat entranced all night, simply listening, and why, when dawn broke, they solemnly chanted:

Buddham charanam gachchami,

Sangham charanam gachchami, Dharmam charanam gachchami.

(I surrender myself to the Buddha, the law, the Sangha).

By declaring this, the 'Three Jewels' (Triratna) of Buddhism, they spontaneously formed the Sangha, or monastic order of Buddhists.

After that, the Buddha's teachings spread all over the fertile Gangetic plain – to King Prasenajit of Kosala, to the Buddha's father, wife and son at Kapilavastu (Rahul joined the Sangha), and the old territories of Vaisali, Sravasti, Rajagriha and Kusinagara.

For forty years the Buddha wandered and preached tirelessly, drawing all manners of converts, from kings, weary of war and suddenly hopeful of peace; to noblemen, traders, farmers, the rich and the poor, whom the new religion treated with beautiful impartiality; the socially oppressed, who could scarcely believe that a casteless option existed, and the legendary courtesan Ambapali, who had been declared state property by her home republic, Vaisali, to put an end to the constant feuding that went on for her favours.

To all these seekers, the Buddha appeared as truly godlike, but he told of his lives as a Bodhisattva (Buddha-to-be) in 547 tales called the *Jataka*, in which he went through animal and human births before he was reborn as Siddhartha. Later Buddhists believe he will be reborn as Maitreya, who will deliver the world from evil once and for all.

But the Buddha's earthly life had to end first. It happened at Kusinagara, when he was an ailing eighty, in a grove of sal trees. He lay on his right side, his head to the north, attended by his faithful disciple of many years, Ananda, and other monks of the Sangha. His last words were, according to the scripture *Digha-nika*, "Work out your salvation with diligence." He was cremated with the honours due to a Chakravartin, a universal monarch. All the kings of the Gangetic plain came to his funeral. His ashes were divided into eight parts, each taken to a different kingdom and enshrined in a domed stupa, a shape derived from his begging bowl.

Though, as some are at pains to point out, when his followers asked the Buddha how they should consecrate his memory, he is said to have silently inverted his bowl to signify 'nothing'. But instead, they chose to so model their temples to him.

After the Buddha's parinirvana (final deliverance) his teachings spread to far kingdoms, with inevitable differences in interpretation. The first and oldest school, Theravada, (the old school) was scathingly called Hinayana, the Lesser Vehicle, by the newer order, Mahayana or Great Vehicle. Buddhist councils were convened by a number of kings in the centuries that followed; first in c. 400 BC by Ajatashatru the parricide, who killed his father Bimbisara for the throne of Magadha, and later two other councils at Vaisali to review rules for the Sangha and for the lay Buddhists.

Early in the 3rd century BC, Megasthenes, the Seleucid Greek ambassador to the court of Chandragupta Maurya wrote in his book *Indika* of the amicable co-existence of the Vedic religion and Buddhism. But while Chandragupta was content to stay a benign Hindu patron of Buddhism, his grandson Ashoka converted, after an emotional cataclysm: in a bid to secure the ports (and profitable southeast Asian trade) of Kalinga (modern Orissa), he had waged a terrible war that left thousands dead or wounded. Overcome by grief at the havoc his ambition had wrought, Ashoka swore to give up violence.

With the true zeal of a new convert, he reorganised his kingdom, appointing Dharma-mahamantras or moral guardians and inscribing his newly-embraced tenets on rocks and pillars all over his vast empire. Ashokan edicts urging non-violence tolerance and vegetarianism have cropped up in places as far apart as Afghanistan, Lumbini (in the Nepal terai), Delhi (where the National Museum boasts a splendid collection of Buddhist art and a fabulous copy of an Ashokan edict in the front garden) – and Sasaram in Bihar.

Moreover, Ashoka patronised 64,000 monks who lived in the viharas (abodes) that mushroomed in Magadha, and held a council of monks at his capital, Pataliputra, the site of modern Patna. The council decided to send missionaries abroad. Exemplary monks set forth to the northern kingdoms of Kashmir and Gandhara and south to what are now Maharashtra and Karnataka.

Ashoka's son and daughter, Mahendra and Sanghamitra, sailed to Sri Lanka, taking along a shoot from the original Bo Tree and won over many converts.

New centres of Buddhist learning developed in Ajanta and Ellora in Maharashtra, Sanchi and Bharhut in central India and especially in Nalanda in the east, where a great university blossomed. The Nalanda University functioned uninterrupted for over a thousand years, until it was razed and pillaged by an invading general, Bakhtiar Khilji, in the 13th century.

Another fillip to Buddhism came from the Kushana king Kanishka (AD 78-101). Kanishka held a major Buddhist council at Jalandhara in Kashmir. Five hundred monks undertook to translate Buddhist scriptures into Sanskrit – the earliest texts of northern Mahayana Buddhism.

And it was under Kanishka's patronage of stupa-builders, artisans and sculptors that the Buddha was first depicted in human form and not just through symbols like the Bo Tree and his footprint. These sculptures, called Mathura-Gandhara art after the southern and northern reaches of Kanishka's empire inspired representational Hindu art in the centuries that followed.

Six centuries after Kanishka, Harsha Vardhana, a powerful north Indian king who ruled from Thaneswar (near Delhi) was almost assassinated by a cabal of brahmins for favouring Xuan Zhuang, a Chinese pilgrim, who, like another Buddhist monk, Fa Hien before him, travelled to India in search of Buddhist manuscripts and to retrace the sacred path of the Buddha from Kapilavastu to Kusinagara. His travelogue tells much about the India of those times.

In what is now the state of Maharashtra, Buddhist monks were excavating caves at Ajanta, Ellora, Udaygiri and Khandgiri and decorating them with exquisite murals. Another great centre of Buddhism existed at Nagarjunakonda, where a great stupa was erected and adorned with sculpture.

Later, the Palas who ruled Bengal and parts of eastern India from the 8th to 12th centuries were also devout Buddhists, and it is in their time that Tantric Buddhism came about. It included elaborate rituals and the use of mysterious diagrams (mandalas) and spells (mantras). A monk named Dipankara Srijnana Atisa took this approach to Tibet, where Mahayana and Tantric belief blended into an esoteric cult called Vajrayana (thunderbolt-vehicle). Another Buddhist scholar from Nalanda, Padmasambhava, introduced Lamaism in Tibet, blending the Mahayana credo with the local Bons religion. He is still worshipped in Tibet as the reborn Boddhisattva Avalokiteswara ('downward looking') and is depicted on beautiful silk *tangkhas*, silk embroidered scrolls and on the rice-paper depictions of the Wheel of Life, its heavens and hells.

From Tibet to Ladakh was no great step for determined monks and soon this mountain province built its own soaring lamaseries, high walled and mysterious, like Thikse, which endures as a living centre of the faith even today.

But the onslaughts of Islam and the increasingly bizarre aspects of Tantric Buddhism, with its devil drums, gongs and frozen hells, turned the common people away from Buddhism around the 13th century. The very land that had joyously welcomed the simple yet challenging doctrine of the Sakyamuni now sought, almost with relief, the direct communication with a personal deity exhorted by the saints of the flowering Bhakti movement. Liberal and casteless, this fresh and vigorous form of Hindu Vaishnavism was often propounded by men of humble origin. They denied the need for priestly middlemen, as the Sakyamuni once had, and sang of a humane, kindly God who loved and forgave, who wanted his children to live in joy and harmony, through good deeds, tolerance and non-violence.

That was the end of official Buddhism on its home ground. But the message endured, retold by new voices with new names. Was that why the Buddha figured so much in the Hindu lore of my childhood? Was that the straightforward reason for his installation as the ninth Avatar of God? When I realized how naturally body and mind moved into gear from the twinkling, flute-playing stance of Krishna, the eigth avatar, to the total stillness of the Buddha's padmasana, it seemed entirely plausible that Sakyamuni was alive in a way no priest nor invading soldier nor worker of black magic could ever fathom.

Tibetan images of the Buddha in Ladakh, in the Himalayas.

Left: Pilgrims at Bodh Gaya, where the Buddha is believed to have attained enlightenment. Above: Buddhist monks gather at Bodh Gaya to pray and to perform religious rituals, on the occasion of Buddha Purnima, which commemorates the birth, enlightenment and death of the Buddha.

Left: A Tibetan image of the Buddha, with offerings of butter-lamps on the altar. Above: Buddhist lamas or monks. Top: An image of a Tibetan Buddhist deity.

Facing page: A mural depicting the Buddha in the Ajanta caves, famed for their extraordinary paintings. Left: A painting from the Ajanta caves representing the Buddha before he gained enlightenment.

Left: The gateway to the great stupa at Sanchi is sculpted with images from Buddhist scriptures. Above: A female figure called a yakshi is used to form the bracket of the gateway at Sanchi.

*Above: A Tibetan image of the
crowned Buddha in Leh.
Right: A Buddhist memorial
in the high altitude desert
region of Ladakh.*

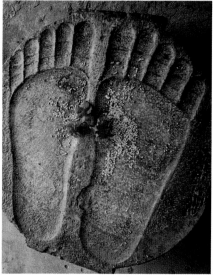

Left: A statue of the Buddha at
Nagarjunakonda, near
Hyderabad. Above: A widely
used symbol for the Buddha
at Bodh Gaya.
Facing page: Richly
ornamented Buddhist
temples are found in
several parts of India, built
by Tibetans, who fled their
country following the Chinese
invasion in the early sixties.

Fairs

Festive Explosions of Colour and Excitement

SHOBITA PUNJA

Left: Colourfully dressed Rajasthani villagers at one of the fairs that punctuate the rural year with excitement and enjoyment.
Above: A Rajasthani folk performer balances a lamp with many flames on her head as she dances.

The experience of India awakens all the senses with its vibrant colours, subtle fragrances, myriad textures and forms, stirring sounds and mouth-watering tastes. And participating in a village fair captures the distinctive spirit of this country. The annual cycle of fairs and festivals are dominated and directed by cosmic movements, following the phases of the moon and the changing relationship of the sun with the earth. Important celebrations occur around the full-moon, moonless nights, and solar equinoxes. The Hindu and Muslim calendars are different from the standard Christian one followed throughout the world, for they are based on the lunar cycle, and the rhythms of agriculture. Festivals such as Pongal, Holi, Teej and Diwali are regulated by the flow of the seasons that culminate in significant agricultural events such as harvest and reaping, sowing and transplanting. Being an agricultural nation of great size and with a wide range of climatic zones there is great diversity in the produce of each region, governed by distinct annual cycles of change and celebrated in a variety of ways depending on the local tradition.

Every region of India offers a different experience, subtle in its variation, though inherently uniform in essence. The festivals and the accompanying melas or fairs range from the gay and flamboyant carnival at Goa in February, where one can see floats and elaborate masks and costumes, to the more sober procession of the Urs at Ajmer, where Muslims from all parts of the sub-continent assemble to pay their respects to the Sufi saint Moin-ud-din Chishti. There are ancient fairs that coincide with the celebration of religious events such as Janmashtami in North India, while in the temple city of Kanchipuram images of Lord Krishna are taken out into the streets in a huge parade, accompanied by devotional music and songs. The immersion of the images of the elephant-headed god Ganesh, patron of auspicious beginnings in Maharashtra and Durga, who symbolises victory over evil and creative strength, in Bengal during their special festivals are also occasions for music and dance. Many festivals are a subtle combination of commerce and spiritual activity.

At the start of the year, between the months of January and February, fairs are organised to celebrate Pongal in the southern states of Andhra Pradesh, Karnataka and Tamil Nadu. The festivities are distinguished by regional, social and family traditions. Most homes are spring-cleaned and decorated for the celebration. Families gather to prepare and eat rice dishes cooked with the freshly harvested crop. In some places in Tamil Nadu, one day is dedicated to all the animals who assist in agricultural labour. The fair grounds, roads and village paths are lined with parading cows and bullocks ornately decorated with tassels and ribbons tied to their horns, paint on their faces and embroidered cloths on their backs. It is a wonderful sight to see these creatures who labour so hard for mankind, being bathed and bedecked for

221

this special day on which they come into their own.

Some melas only take place at a specific place, every six or twelve years. The mythical story around the Kumbha mela, describes how the world was created and how the gods and demons fought over a jar of amrit, ambrosia, the nectar of immortality. One of the gods was able to snatch away the jar of amrit but he was pursued by the demons. As he flew across the skies to safety, a few drops of the nectar of immortality fell into the waters at Prayag (Allahabad), Haridwar, Nasik and Ujjain. Since twelve years is considered equivalent to one god-year, the event of spilling-the-jar (Kumbha) of amrit is celebrated once in a cycle of twelve years. Having waited twelve long years for this most holy and auspicious time, thousands of people from all parts of India come to bathe in these waters, made holy by the amrit, in the hope of attaining salvation and eternal life.

As if to compensate for the long wait, the Ardha (half) Kumbha mela is organised every six years at Allahabad, the confluence of the rivers Ganga, Yamuna and the invisible Sarasvati. It is truly an incredible sight to see an estimated two million people assemble on the banks of the river to bathe. The old, helped by the young, children hoisted on their fathers' shoulders, women in traditional clothes, naked ascetics and colourfully attired mendicants, famous religious gurus or leaders carried in decorated palanquins by their devotees, all making their way to the river at the appointed time. The air is thick with dust, whipped up by trampling feet, the shrill sound of devotional music filling the sky as if to carry the devotees' prayers up to the heavens. The crowds follow an invisible order of movement and there is rarely a stampede, since everyone is engrossed in performing their individual form of worship and prayer. After the ritual bath and the offering of prayers, the devotees move away from the river to allow others to worship. The flow of the crowds to and from the water, is regulated by bamboo rails and fences. After bathing, the pilgrims dress in their finest attire and roam the fair-grounds, where there are temporary stalls selling food, decorative items and religious images for the home.

To this list must be added the modern fairs created to serve the tourist industry in the country, the Jaisalmer Desert Festival now held in January-February and the Surajkund Crafts Mela in February, in the state of Haryana, are all attempts to recapture and preserve the spirit of India by providing patronage to local craftsmen and artists. They draw large number of visitors, as traditional fairs always have done.

Last year, I was able to attend the Maha-Shivratri mela at Khajuraho in the state of Madhya Pradesh. This religious festival is associated with Shiva, the Lord of Creation and also of Universal Destruction. (For everything that is created, by nature's law, will ultimately die.) Maha-Shivratri is celebrated in all the great centres of Shaivite worship such as Mandi, Banaras (Varanasi), Ujjain, Bombay, Mysore and Rameshvaram. Yet these festivals have a distinct city-flavour and their beauty has been overshadowed by the loud speaker, film music, nylon tinsel and glitter. Khajuraho is a small village with over twenty magnificent temples built in the tenth and eleventh centuries. Though a tourist site of great popularity, the village has preserved its inherent quality and is a charming sleepy little place, surrounded by fields nestling amidst a rugged landscape. On the day before Maha-Shivratri, the village was quiet and peaceful and the local inhabitants were busy with their daily tasks. Around three in the morning, strange rumbling sounds could be heard, as hundreds of bullock carts filled with pilgrims made their way to Khajuraho. By day-break every open space in the village was occupied by the carts parked neatly in rows. The devotees had come with their entire families, old parents, children in arms, brothers and sisters. They had fasted the previous night and had travelled from their distant villages in the cool dark hours to arrive at Khajuraho by dawn. As the sun rose, long lines of people made their way towards the sacred Shiv Sagar tank.

After their worship, the pilgrims returned to their carts and dressed. It was then time to visit the mela, held at the village fair grounds.

There is a certain established order in the display of wares at this and other melas across the country. Like the ancient caravansarais set up by the traders all along the silk-route from China to the Middle East, there is usually a recognisable plan for the temporary market place. Vendors selling food occupy one area, the hardware stalls another, agricultural tools are set up at the other end. The villager who comes to buy can find in one section of the fair a number of stalls selling similar items and can then choose and bargain till he is satisfied with the object and its price. The assembly of stalls is also ruled by caste laws, visibly followed in the layout of the mela. The potter and leather worker are relegated to the fringe of the fair, as they belong to the lowest caste and are forced by their profession to work with materials that are considered unclean. Visitors go from one section to the other buying all they need.

The village mela is a virtual parade ground for traditional Indian crafts. In these handmade objects one can see timeless designs that are a perfect synthesis of form and function. The list of skills displayed at the fair give you a glimpse of the creativity of rural India. The crafts of each region are distinctly designed to meet specific needs and produced out of locally available material. In the fairs of Manipur and the north-eastern regions of India, a variety of household objects with the most sophisticated designs are produced out of bamboo. In the fairs of Rajasthan and Gujarat, items made out of camel wool and riding equipment are found in plenty. The fairs also sell crafts that belong exclusively to that region. Children's toys are a speciality of all fairs throughout the country.

The mela also offers entertainment for the entire family. Acrobats, jugglers, folk musicians and puppeteers are all part of a mela. There are bawdy shows, dance performances by the Hijras, eunuch entertainers dressed in flashy female attire, wriggling their hips in an attempt to attract an audience. Often a theatre company comes to perform in the evening at the mela. Most famous of the theatre forms associated with festivals is the Ramlila of Ramnagar, held during the Dussehra celebrations on the outskirts of Banaras.

Since the mood of the mela is transitory and fleeting, the art of display, of advertising wares is often innovative and ingenious. A man selling hair ribbons and necklaces, for example, may have a portable shop. A large black umbrella becomes a canopy and the wire frame inside the umbrella serves as hanging racks from which ribbons of many colours flutter in the breeze. The tattoo artist frequently carries with him a little battery operated box. His entire repertoire of tattoo designs may be punctured along the surface of his forearm. As young girls sit beside him to discuss designs, he will display his arms, suggesting where each motif may be placed on the wrist, arm, leg, neck, cheek and forehead. Another man strings yards of chains and necklaces on his fingers, waving his wares in your face as you walk by. When the mela is over, closing shop is easy and the vendor is ready to move on to the next mela.

The month of Phalgun, between February and March, is a time for several festivals, for it marks the end of winter and almost overnight, after Maha-Shivratri, the landscape of northern and central India is ablaze with the colour of flowering trees and the fragrance of mango blossoms. Soon it is time to celebrate the arrival of spring. Human beings strive to imitate the wonders of the season by splashing coloured powder and water on their families and friends at the festival of Holi, associated with Lord Krishna. Fairs are held in many villages and towns of north India. In devotional literature, music and dance, Krishna is described as an endearing, naughty child always up to tricks and pranks, as the cowherd who played with the gopis and as the divine lover of Radha, his beautiful friend and companion. Songs, poems and miniature paintings of the region have immortalised the suggestive love-play of Krishna and Radha as they play Holi, spraying colours and water. The Holi celebrations are especially elaborate at Mathura, which is closely associated with Lord Krishna, and several melas are held in this area.

For the farmer, it is harvest time. The fields of ripening wheat in the Punjab begin to look like carpets of gold. At Anandpur, Hola Mohalla is celebrated by the Nihang Sikhs. A great gathering of Nihangs, arriving on their magnificent stallions and carts, results in a fair of massive proportions. Tent-pegging, archery and fencing competitions are held for the participants. It is the scene of animated activity with a valiant display of combat skills and martial arts.

As the summer wears on, the heat stills the passion to celebrate and the scorching sun makes it impossible to travel. In the cooler pastures of Himachal and Uttarakhand summer agricultural fairs take place around this time. The Hemis festival and fair in Ladakh in July takes place when the high moutain passes and trade routes are opened once again. The fairs are accompanied by music and dance, both secular and religious.

The advent of the rains is always a cause for joy and festivity. This period is also associated with the rivers swelling with the melting snows and great river festivals are organised throughout the land. Ganga Dussehra, Teej, Naga Panchami, the Kaveri river festival and Onam with its extravagant boat races along the back waters of Kerala are some of the important events of this season.

The festivals of Dussehra and Diwali herald the coming of the winter, the shortening days and long dark nights are celebrated with lamps, lights and fireworks. There are several myths and gods associated with these festivals. Dussehra and Diwali are also associated with the worship of the great female goddesses, Lakshmi, of good fortune and material prosperity, Durga, the Creative Power and the destroyer of evil. In every town in Bengal one can see images of Durga being made, and stalls and shops are lined with statues of this great goddess for sale and eventually for immersion.

It is that time of the year when one invites the blessing of Lakshmi, and it is the best time of year to buy jewellery and household goods. It is a time to test one's good luck and fortune. Gambling, feasting and drinking are part of the festivities of the season. It is a time also for music and dance. The story of the *Ramayana* is closely linked to Diwali celebrations. It is on the moonless night between the months of October and November that Lord Rama returned victorious from Lanka, having rescued his wife from Ravana and completed his fourteen years of exile from his kingdom. Fairs and melas are held throughout the country to commemorate this great annual event. Houses in every corner of India are decorated on the evening of Diwali, so that Rama can find his way back to his rightful throne in the heart and home of each devotee.

The full moon night, purnima, in the month of Kartik in the Hindu calender, falls between the months of October and November and is considered one of the most auspicious times of the year. Several places in India celebrate Kartik Purnima in their individual way. Most spectacular and different from the other religious fairs are the cattle fairs of Pushkar and Jhalawar in Rajasthan and Sonepur in Bihar.

The Sonepur cattle fair is a wonderful event. Situated on a confluence of the holy Ganges river, the mela draws many visitors though it is not so well known to tourists. The most spectacular part of this ancient fair is the trade in elephants. These magnificent creatures, largely from the jungles of north-eastern India, are sold to the forest department, farmers and temples throughout the country.

In the desert state of Rajasthan, near the city of Ajmer, is Pushkar, one of the holiest and most unusual places of pilgrimage. The Pushkar lake and over 400 temples in the town and on the neighbouring hillside, are considered to be of great mythological significance. At Pushkar is one of the rare temples dedicated to Brahma, the Creator of the Universe. In the myth we are told that on one occasion Brahma told a lie. Shiva cursed him, declaring that no temple was to be built in his honour. However, at Pushkar, Brahma destroyed several demons, killing them with his lotus flower. Where the petals fell, holy lakes appeared. It was beside the Pushkar lake that Brahma also performed a great sacrifice to which he invited all the gods and goddesses. To commemorate this event people from all over come to bathe in the holy lake to wash away their sins, as Brahma did. The story goes on to say that while Brahma was praying, his wife Savitri failed to appear and perform her part of the rituals, so Brahma married a tribal Gujar girl called Gayatri. To this fair come thousands of Gujars and other tribal and rural folk of Rajasthan. For, apart from the holy dip and the prayers, it is also the time to buy and sell cattle, horses and camels.

The site of the fair is magical as the grey mist of early morning rises slowly over thousands of tents and camels. As the day progresses, the colourful garments and the turbans of the Rajasthani men obliterate the dullness of their natural sandy habitat. Flowering skirts of many colours, turbans with dyed design, embroidered waist-coats, and sequinned slippers of amazing designs compete for one's attention and admiration. The clothes of these people, who live in such dreary surroundings of sand dunes and cactus, are vibrantly coloured and decorated with patterns of flowers, plants, peacocks and rivers. The camels at the fair are especially well groomed, some with their coats clipped to form beautiful designs. But camels are not the only attraction at the fair. Artists and musicians from near and far, come to liven up the mela at Pushkar. The bard, the story teller and the puppeteer, playing on their simple stringed instruments, draw out the melody of Pushkar long after the colours of the dusk fade into the night sky. The nomadic lifestyle of these colourful people, their art and culture has made the Pushkar fair a great tourist attraction. Perhaps it is the innate nomadic spirit of all human beings that draws them to such haunting experiences.

Preceding page: At the Rath Yatra festival, enormous wooden temple carts carrying images of Lord Jagannath are taken out in procession in the town of Puri. The word juggernaut has its origin in the overwhelming, unstoppable power of these enormous temples on wheels. Left: Images of the wicked king Ravana are set alight at the festival of Dussehra which celebrates the victory of the god-king Rama and the triumph of good over evil. Above: A child actor dressed as Lakshman, Rama's brother, at the Ramnagar Ramlila, Banaras.

229

Facing page: A Bengali priest conducts ritual worship of the goddess Durga during the Durga Puja festival in eastern India.
Left: The elephant-headed god Ganesha being taken out in procession during the festival of Ganesha Chaturthi in Maharashtra.

Left: A procession of sumptuously decorated elephants is the highlight of the annual festival at the magnificent temple at Trichur in Kerala. Above: A decorated elephant and his keeper on their way to join the procession at the Trichur temple.

Left: Snake worship at the festival of Nagapanchami in Maharashtra. Above: A circus from Orissa at the Pushkar Fair in Rajasthan draws crowds of colourfully dressed local people.

Left, above: Holi, the festival of colour is celebrated all over north India in honour of Lord Krishna.
Left: Diwali, the festival of lights.

Left, above: A procession during the festival of Teej in Jaipur, Rajasthan. Left: Tazias at Moharrum. Tazias are replicas of the tombs of the Prophet's grandsons Hussain and Hassan.

The annual snake boat races in Kerala are an eagerly awaited event.

Photographers Credits

Pages 1-7 : M.D. Sharma, 1; Rajesh Bedi, 2-3 double spread, 4-5 double spread, 6-7 double spread.

Pages 8-15 : Ashok Dilwali, 8-9 double spread; Jagdish Agrawal/Fotomedia 10-11 double spread; Shalini Saran, 12; Courtesy National Museum, 13.

Pages 16-23 : Ajay Khullar, 16; Rajesh Bedi, 17; Ashok Dilwali, 23.

Pages 24-31 : Rajesh Bedi, 24-25 double spread, 28-29 double spread, 31 right; Ashok Dilwali, 26-27 double spread, 27 right; D.J. Singh, 30-31 double spread.

Pages 32-39 : Ashok Dilwali, 32 left, 32-33 double spread, 36-37 double spread; D.J. Singh, 34-35 double spread, 35 right; Rajesh Bedi, 38, 39

Pages 40-47 : Rajesh Bedi, 44-45 double spread; 47 right; Ashok Dilwali, 46-47 double spread.

Pages 48-55 : Rajesh Bedi, 48 left, 48-49 double spread, 50-51 double spread, 51 right, 52 left, 52-53 double spread, 54-55 double spread.

Pages 56-63 : Rajesh Bedi, 56-57 double spread, 57 right, 58,59, 60-61 double spread, 62, 63.

Pages 64-71 : Shalini Saran, 68-69 double spread; M.D. Sharma, 70-71 double spread; Gopi Gajwani, 71 right.

Pages 72-79 : Rajesh Bedi, 72-73 double spread, 73 right, 76-77 double spread, 78, 79; S. Mitra, 74 left; Sondeep Shankar, 74-75 double spread.

Pages 80-87 : M.D. Sharma, 80-81 double spread; D.J. Singh, 81 right; R.K. Gaur, 82 left, 82-83 double spread; Rajesh Bedi, 84; P.K. De, 85; S.N. Sharma, 86; Shalini Saran, 87.

Pages 88-95 : Gopi Gajwani, 88-89 double spread, 92; S.N. Sharma, 89 right; Ashok Dilwali, 90-91 double spread; Sondeep Shankar, 93.

Pages 96-103 : Gopi Gajwani, 98-99 double spread, 99 right, below, 102-103 double spread; Ashok Dilwali, 99 right, above, 100-101 double spread; Bhawani Shankar, 102 left.

Pages 104-111 : D.N. Dubey, 104-105 double spread; Sondeep Shankar, 106-107 double spread; Rajesh Bedi, 108, 109.

Pages 112-119 : D.N. Dubey, 115, 118-119 double spread; Rajesh Bedi, 116-117 double spread.

Pages 120-127 : Kamal Sahai, 120, 126-127 double spread; Gopi Gajwani, 121, 125, 127 right; D.N. Dubey, 122-123 double spread, 123 right; Rajesh Bedi, 124.

Pages 128-135 : Rajesh Bedi, 128-129 double spread, 130,131.

Pages 136-143 : P.K. De, 137, 140-141 double spread, 142-143 double spread; Rajesh Bedi, 138-139 double spread, 139 right.

Pages 144-151 : Pramod Mistry, 144-145 double spread, 145 right; Darshan Lall, 146, 147; Amar Talwar/Fotomedia, 148 left; Ajay Khullar/Fotomedia, 148-149 double spread; Aditya Arya/Fotomedia, 150; Rajesh Bedi, 151.

Pages 152-159 : Rajesh Bedi, 152-153 double spread, 154; P.K. De, 155.

Pages 160-167 : Shalini Saran, 161; Ashok Dilwali, 162-163 double spread; Rajesh Bedi, 164-165 double spread, 165 right, 166, 167.

Pages 168-175 : P.K. De, 168-169 double spread, 169 right; Rajesh Bedi, 170-171 double spread, 171 right, 174; Ajaya Khullar, 172-173 double spread; Courtesy National Museum, 175.

Pages 176-183 : Rajesh Bedi, 181, 182-183 double spread.

Pages 184-191 : Rajesh Bedi, 184-185 double spread, 186, 188, 189; P.K. De, 187 left; Shalini Saran, 187 right; Avinash Pasricha, 190-191 double spread.

Pages 192-199 : Avinash Pasricha, 192; D.N. Dubey, 193; Rajesh Bedi, 194, 195; Ajay Khullar, 196,197; P.K. De, 198-199 double spread.

Pages 200-207 : Aditya Arya, 200; D.J. Singh, 201; Ashok Dilwali, 207.

Pages 208-215 : Aditya Arya, 208-209 double spread; P.K. De, 209 right; D.J. Singh, 210-211 double spread, 211 right; Rajesh Bedi, 212, 213; R.K. Gaur, 214-215 double spread, 215 right.

Pages 216-223 : D.J. Singh, 216 left; Rajesh Bedi, 216-217 double spread, 220; Ashok Dilwali, 218; D.N. Dubey, 219 left; P.K. De, 219 right; Avinash Pasricha, 221.

Pages 224-231 : D.N. Dubey, 226-227 double spread; Rajesh Bedi, 228-229 double spread, 229 right, 231; Ajay Khullar, 230.

Pages 232-239 : Rajesh Bedi, 232-233 double spread, 234, 235; Shalini Saran, 233 right, 237 above; Bindu Arora/Fotomedia, 236, above; Sondeep Shankar, 236, below; Gopi Gajwani, 237, below; Ashok Dilwali, 238-239 double spread.

Captions

(Pages 1-11)

Page 1 : A stained glass window depicting Lord Ganesha, the elephant-headed god of auspicious beginnings.

Pages 2-3 : Pilgrims travel from distant corners of India to Banaras, holiest of Indian cities. Priests seated under palm-leaf umbrellas, on the banks of the river Ganga help devotees to perform religious rituals.

Pages 4-5 : Ajmer, in Rajasthan, is a centre of pilgrimage to followers of the Islamic faith in India.

Pages 6-7 : At nightfall, lamps suspended on these poles, in wicker baskets, will be lit. It is believed that they light the path of the dead. This ritual is one of many age-old practices which are still observed in the city of Banaras, beside the holy Ganga.

Pages 8-9 : Temple bells at a shrine that looks out on the eternal snows of the Himalayas. This great range of mountains is considered the abode of the gods.

Pages 10-11 : At sunset the stone temples at Khajuraho take on compelling beauty.